SOUS VIDE COOKING
with SANSAIRE

RECIPES FOR UNMATCHED FLAVOR

SOUS VIDE COOKING
with SANSAIRE

Compatible with all sous vide immersion devices

RECIPES FOR UNMATCHED FLAVOR

FRONT TABLE BOOKS | AN IMPRINT OF CEDAR FORT, INC. | SPRINGVILLE, UTAH

ISBN 13: 978-1-4621-2068-0

Published by Front Table Books, an imprint of Cedar Fort, Inc.
2373 W. 700 S., Springville, UT 84663
Distributed by Cedar Fort, Inc., www.cedarfort.com

LIBRARY OF CONGRESS CATALOGING-IN-PUBLICATION DATA

Names: Modern Chef, Inc.
Title: Sous vide cooking with Sansaire : recipes for unmatched flavor /
    Modern Chef, Inc.
Description: Springville, Utah : Front Table Books, an imprint of Cedar Fort,
    Inc., [2017] | Includes index.
Identifiers: LCCN 2017029133 (print) | LCCN 2017031105 (ebook) | ISBN
    9781462128204 (epub and mobi) | ISBN 9781462120680 (perfect binding :
    acid-free paper)
Subjects: LCSH: Sous-vide cooking. | LCGFT: Cookbooks.
Classification: LCC TX690.7 (ebook) | LCC TX690.7 .S68 2017 (print) | DDC
    641.5/87--dc23
LC record available at https://lccn.loc.gov/2017029133

Cover and page design by M. Shaun McMurdie
Cover design © 2017 Cedar Fort, Inc.
Edited by Jessica Romrell & Chelsea Holdaway

Printed in the United States of America

10 9 8 7 6 5 4 3 2 1

Printed on acid-free paper

SCAN to visit

www.sansaire.com

We dedicate this cookbook to you and all the other home chefs
who still enjoy the experience of flipping through paper pages and
hunting for ideas for the next culinary adventure.

We would like to acknowledge with extreme gratitude
all of the people involved in bringing this book to life:
Geoff Adleman, Zach Adleman, Geoffrey Barker, Jessica Cnossen,
Kati Gonzales, Motoko Hayashi, Cindy Hernandez, Johnna
Hobgood, Lynnette Husted, Jason Solomon,
Lukas Svec, and Liz Wilson.

Contents

Introduction.. 1

How to Use the Immersion Method............................. 5

Appetizers.. 7

Breakfast and Brunch...41

Entrées..69

Sides.. 123

Soups & Salads 157

Desserts.. 183

Beverages...203

About the Chefs and Photographer..................... 214

Index... 216

Introduction

My first interaction with sous vide cooking started with me doing a web search on how to pronounce it. It turns out it was as easy as saying "sue-veed," and it is simply French for "under vacuum." I was shocked to discover I had enjoyed sous vide cooked meals on numerous occasions without knowing it. It is the best-kept secret in fine dining. Ever wonder why your steak and chicken come out perfectly cooked not long after you ordered them? Or how some restaurants deliver the best-looking (and tasting) poached egg to your table? Chances are high that they used sous vide.

Since you are reading this book, you have already taken a major step in doing this on your own.

Sous vide cooking uses precise temperature control to achieve perfect results every time. These results are repeatable and delicious and they are hard to duplicate through any other cooking method. Foods are cooked evenly from edge to edge, to the exact doneness you want. And, because foods won't overcook, your meal is ready when you are. The world's best chefs rely on sous vide, and now you can too.

Tender, juicy, and perfectly cooked from edge to edge.

Gray and overcooked around the edges. Squeezed dry from high heat.

On a stovetop, in an oven, or on a grill, you're cooking with temperatures that are much higher than you ever want your food to reach. If you turn your back for a moment too long, your steak can end up as a tough, gray mess. And, even if you do achieve a medium-rare interior, the high heat environment of traditional cooking creates bands of overcooked areas around the outside.

To cook sous vide, all you'll need are four items.

FIRST, you will need a vessel to hold your water. This can be your favorite pot, ice chest, or even your kitchen sink. You read that correctly, you just need to plug your sink and fill it. I have seen 45 perfectly poached eggs created during a cooking class. Another favorite story involves using a hotel ice bucket and enjoying a perfectly cooked steak while on a business trip (without leaving the room).

SECOND, you will need an immersion circulator. This is the fancy name for our Sansaire device that happens to be among the most powerful consumer-focused devices on the market. Our circulator has the best form and function, and is capable of the level of precision needed for flawless sous vide cooking. Simply clip your circulator to the side of your cooking vessel.

THIRD, fill your cooking vessel with fresh tap water. This is a great time to power your unit on and get the temperature rising. Set it to the desired level specified in the recipe.

FOURTH, put your food into either a plastic bag or canning jar*. In the case of eggs, they come with a natural container, and the shell works just fine. Zip-top plastic bags** are perfectly safe to use in sous vide water baths.

In the end, the sous vide method of cooking will change the way you spend time in the kitchen. It allows for

- Unattended cooking—you don't need to be tethered to your stove

- Simplified timing—no more split-second timing to get your doneness just right

- Perfect results—no guesswork, just edge-to-edge perfection

- Convenience—no mess, easy to make ahead

I am now well past the days of web searching the pronunciation of sous vide and am knee-deep in exploring the many recipes (most contained in this very book) that take advantage of this method of cooking. I hope these recipes, particularly the steak and salmon recipes, are a gateway for your transition to sous vide cooking. Replicating fine-dining in your own kitchen is an awesome experience, but there is so much more. I challenge you to explore the various recipes in this book and fully experience the entire spectrum of what sous vide can do.

It is my pleasure to welcome you to sous vide cooking. Explore it, embrace it, and enjoy it!

— **SANSAIRE**

* The canning jar tends to be the best container for recipes like our Chocolate Espresso Cheesecake or Cara Cara Orange Flan. The jar also allows easy transportation of the finished food making you the rock star at any party when you show up with exquisite dessert in 8-ounce glass jars.

** Check the bags' nutrition label to ensure they're BPA-free, PVC-free, and are made from polyethylene and polypropylene. We always recommend using freezer-style bags for sous vide cooking because they're made from thicker plastic with stronger construction. They'll hold up to boiling temperatures, which are well beyond most sous vide cooking temperatures.

If you have a vacuum sealer, those bags are even better. For cooking times longer than 8 hours, we recommend vacuum sealing, mostly to ensure that your bags don't float, but for everything else, zip-top plastic bags work great! Although you can use any resealable plastic bag, we recommend using brand name zip-top bags.

How to Use the Immersion Method

If you aren't using a vacuum sealer, seal using the immersion method. With the top of the bag slightly open on one side, use tongs to carefully submerge the bag into the bottom of the water bath, without allowing any water into the bag itself. The pressure of the water circulating around the outside of the bag will push any air out and form a seal around the food. Using the side of the water container, carefully seal the bag.

Appetizers

Baccala

SERVES 6–8

Baccala is a classic Italian dish with a wonderful mix of intense herbs and salt cod flavors. We use salt cod in this recipe, but feel free to substitute fresh cod. It will be moist and tender and blow your mind in ways that traditional Italian baccala recipes can't replicate. Because fish is so delicate, small differences in cooking temperature have a big impact on the final texture. Leave nothing to chance by using sous vide.

2 lbs. boneless salt cod

⅓ cup extra virgin olive oil

3 cloves garlic, finely chopped

¼ cup fresh Italian parsley, finely chopped

2 tsp. crushed red pepper

1   Soak salt cod in water in the refrigerator for 2 days. Rinse well and change the water every 8 hours. Skip this step if substituting fresh cod.

2   Preheat the water bath to 131°F (55°C).

3   Pat the fish dry. Seal the fish and olive oil in a plastic bag using the immersion method or a vacuum sealer, ensuring that the fish forms a single layer. Submerge the bag in the water bath and cook for 30 minutes.

4   Remove cod from the water bath, drain liquid and pat dry with a paper towel.

5   In a mixing bowl, flake cod into small pieces with a fork. Mix in garlic, parsley, and crushed red pepper. Serve at room temperature.

Baked Camembert Cheese

RECIPE BY
GEOFFREY BARKER

An easy way to enhance your charcuterie board is by adding this flavorful sous vide Camembert cheese wheel infused with rosemary, sea salt, bay leaves, and honey. It also pairs well with champagne.

1   Preheat the water bath to 95°F (35°C).

2   Lightly score the cheese in a crisscross pattern, just penetrating the skin. Sprinkle salt over the cheese, drizzle with honey, and place herbs on top.

3   Seal the cheese in a plastic bag using the immersion method or a vacuum sealer. Submerge the bag in the water bath and cook for 1 hour.

4   Remove the cheese and gently pat dry the excess moisture. Serve with your favorite accompaniments.

1 wheel Camembert cheese

½ tsp. sea salt

1 tsp. honey

3 sprigs fresh rosemary

2 bay leaves

Buffalo Chicken Wings

SERVES 2

Chicken wings are a favorite party snack. For a slightly healthier twist on traditional recipes, sous vide wings or chicken breast strips instead of frying them. In this recipe, we used traditional Buffalo style hot sauce.

1 Preheat the water bath to 149°F (65°C).

2 Seal the chicken in a plastic bag using the immersion method or a vacuum sealer, ensuring that the chicken wings form a single layer. Submerge the bag in the water bath and cook for 90 minutes.

3 About 10 minutes before the chicken is done, mix the pepper sauce, butter, vinegar, Sansaire Steak Aging Sauce, cayenne pepper, and garlic powder in a bowl.

4 Remove the chicken from the sous vide water bath, drain excess liquid from the bag, and pat chicken dry with a paper towel.

5 Roll each chicken piece in the pepper mixture until fully coated. Serve with celery sticks and blue cheese dressing.

1 lb. chicken wings

⅔ cup hot pepper sauce

½ cup cold unsalted butter, melted

1½ Tbsp. white vinegar

¼ tsp. Sansaire Steak Aging Sauce

⅛ tsp. cayenne pepper

⅛ tsp. garlic powder

4 celery stocks, washed and cut into 3-inch pieces

½ cup blue cheese dressing

Chawan Mushi-Pan (Savory Japanese Egg Custard)

RECIPE BY
MOTOKO HAYASHI

SERVES 4

Chawan Mushi is a savory traditional Japanese egg custard appetizer. "Chawan" means "bowls" and "mushi" means "steamed," but in this case, it's cooked sous vide in a canning jar. Use Sansaire to achieve a smooth creamy texture without fear of overcooking. This light and fluffy custard makes for a perfect appetizer.

1   Preheat the water bath to 176°F (80°C).

2   In a small bowl, combine the dashi broth, soy sauce, and salt.

3   In a separate bowl, beat the eggs then add in the dashi broth and soy sauce mixture, strain it.

4   On the bottom of each jar, place 2–3 pieces of chicken, a mitsuba stem, a shiitake mushroom, shimeji mushrooms, and carrots. Slowly pour the egg mixture in the jars.

5   Seal each jar, but do not tighten completely. The ring should be slightly loose to allow air to escape. Place jars in the water bath, ensuring the water level covers the jars. Cook for 60 minutes.

6   Garnish with a mitsuba leaf. Serve immediately.

1¼ cups dashi (konbu broth) or 1¼ cups water with 1 tsp. dashi powder, at room temperature

2 tsp. soy sauce

⅕ tsp. salt

2 eggs

4 (8-oz.) canning jars

½ small chicken thigh, cut into 1-inch cubes

4 mitsuba stems

4 small shiitake mushrooms, 1-inch in diameter

1 cup shimeji mushrooms

1 carrot, sliced into pieces ⅛-inch thick, cut like a flower

Mitsuba leaf, Japanese parsley or spinach, cut into 1-inch length, for garnish

Cola Pork Belly

SERVES 4

RECIPE BY
MOTOKO HAYASHI

For a surprising twist on pork belly, try this sous vide cola pork belly. The cola keeps the pork belly tender, making for a delicious meal.

1   Preheat the water bath to 140°F (60°C).

2   Combine the mirin, soy sauce, sake, cola, and salt in a plastic bag. Add green onions, ginger, and pork belly.

3   Seal the bag using the immersion method or a vacuum sealer. Place the bag in the water bath to cook for at least 24 hours.

4   Remove the meat from the bag. Reserve the liquid. Heat half of the reserved liquid in a sauce pan and sear the meat on all sides.

5   To serve, pour the sauce over the meat.

2 lbs. pork belly, skin-on or skin-off, cut into 2-inch pieces

1 cup mirin, Japanese cooking wine

1 cup soy sauce

½ cup Japanese sake

2 cups cola

½ tsp. kosher salt

4 green onions, whole

3 slices fresh ginger root

Daikon Cheesesteak

SERVES 4

RECIPE BY
MOTOKO HAYASHI

For a small appetizer that packs a punch, try our sous vide daikon cheesesteak. With Sansaire, the radishes retain their crunchy texture without turning to mush when cooked.

1   Preheat the water bath to 183°F (83.9°C).

2   Seal daikon, chicken broth, and soy sauce in a plastic bag using the immersion method or a vacuum sealer. Place the bag in the sous vide bath for 60 minutes.

3   Remove the daikon from the bag. Season it with salt and pepper. Reserve ¼ cup of the liquid from bag.

4   Heat the oil in a pan and sear the daikon. After one side has been seared, flip it, season it, and place a slice of cheese on each daikon slice. Add the daikon liquid to the pan and cover with a lid.

5   Once the cheese has melted, garnish with parsley. Serve immediately.

1 lb. daikon radishes, sliced ¾-inch thick

1½ cups chicken broth

2 tsp. soy sauce

Salt and pepper to taste

1 Tbsp. olive oil

3 oz. hot pepper jack cheese, thinly sliced

Parsley, chopped

Garlic and Cambozola Cheese Spread

SERVES 4

Sous vide garlic and Cambozola cheese spread on seared naan creates a flavor explosion that is addictive.

1 Preheat the water bath to 190°F (87°C).

2 Slice the top off of a head of garlic and place it in the canning jar. Cover garlic with olive oil. Seal the jar, but do not tighten completely. The ring should be slightly loose to allow air to escape. Add it to the water bath, ensuring the water level covers the jar. Cook for 4 hours or overnight.

3 About 30 minutes before serving, lower the temperature of the water bath to 167°F (75°C). Soften Cambozola cheese by removing rind and placing cheese in a canning jar. Seal jar as instructed in step 2. Cook for 15 minutes.

4 While the cheese is softening in the water bath, warm the naan. Remove jars from the water bath and combine cheese and garlic cloves in a small bowl. Serve with naan bread.

1 head of garlic

1 (8-oz.) canning jar

½ cup olive oil

Canning jar for cheese

4 oz. Cambozola cheese

1 package naan

Garlic Hummus

SERVES 2

Hummus is a delicious Middle Eastern staple. It's a healthy appetizer and snack served with raw carrots, broccoli, snap peas or other vegetables, and sliced pita bread. We soak dried chickpeas in water then sous vide cook them to prep them for our favorite hummus recipe.

1 Place chickpeas in a bowl. Fill bowl with water until the water level is a few inches above the chickpeas. Soak dried chickpeas in refrigerator 12–20 hours or until soft.

2 Preheat the water bath to 194°F (90°C).

3 Remove chickpeas from soaking water, strain, and rinse. Seal chickpeas with fresh water in a plastic bag using the immersion method or a vacuum sealer. Submerge the bag in the water bath and cook for 3½ hours.

4 Remove the chickpeas from the bath, drain water, and chill over ice.

5 In a food processor, add 2 Tbsp. olive oil, lemon juice, garlic cloves, and tahini to the chickpeas. Pulsate, and add water if needed to achieve the desired hummus texture.

6 Transfer to serving bowl and drizzle with remaining olive oil. Sprinkle cumin on top of the hummus. Serve with vegetables and sliced pita bread.

1½ cups dried chickpeas

2½ Tbsp. olive oil, divided

¼ cup fresh lemon juice

2 small or 1 large garlic clove(s), peeled and sliced

¼ cup tahini

1 tsp. ground cumin

Mozzarella Cheese Stuffed Meatballs

SERVES 4–6, YIELDS 24 MEATBALLS

RECIPE BY
MOTOKO HAYASHI

For a crowd-pleasing appetizer, try our sous vide mozzarella stuffed meatballs.

1 Preheat the water bath to 140°F (60°C).

2 In a large mixing bowl, combine the beef, panko, egg, parsley, Parmesan, salt, pepper, onion, and garlic. Mix well and divide into 24.

3 Wrap each mozzarella cheese ball with the meat mixture, forming balls 1½ inches in diameter.

4 Seal the meatballs in a plastic bag using the immersion method or a vacuum sealer. Place the bag in the water bath for 90 minutes. If the meatballs stick together, carefully separate them.

5 Heat olive oil in a large nonstick skillet over medium heat and sauté the cooked meatballs until they are brown. Remove from heat, set aside.

6 Serve with your favorite tomato sauce. Garnish with parsley and Parmesan.

1½ lbs. lean ground beef, preferably 85 percent lean

3 Tbsp. panko (bread crumbs)

1 large egg

¼ cup chopped Italian parsley, plus more for garnish

2 Tbsp. grated Parmesan cheese, plus more for garnish

¾ tsp. salt

½ tsp. ground black pepper

½ onion, minced

2 garlic cloves, minced

24 small fresh mozzarella cheese balls

1 Tbsp. olive oil

Onion Farce (Stuffed Onions)

SERVES 2

RECIPE BY
MOTOKO HAYASHI

Sous vide onion farce makes for a beautiful and delicious appetizer that is sure to impress your dinner guests. It can be made in advance and stored in the fridge.

1   Preheat the water bath to 186.8°F (86°C).

2   Remove the top inch of each onion, mince, and place aside. Reserve 2 tsp.

3   Slightly trim the stalk end of the onions so that the onions will sit flat.

4   Remove inner onion layers, leaving 2–3 of the outer layers.

5   In a small bowl, mix the minced onions, ground meat, garlic, panko, Parmesan cheese, sage, thyme, salt, and pepper.

6   Fill each onion cup with beef mixture. Seal the onion cups with a small amount of broth in a plastic bag using the immersion method or a vacuum sealer. Place the bag in the water for 1 hour.

7   To serve, place the onion in a bowl and pour your favorite consommé over it. Sprinkle Parmesan cheese on top and torch it to brown. Garnish with chervil or parsley and serve.

2 small sweet onions, 2½ inches in diameter

⅓ cup ground beef or ground chicken

¼ tsp. garlic, minced

2 tsp. panko (breadcrumbs)

1 tsp. grated Parmesan cheese, plus more for garnish

¼ tsp. fresh sage, chopped

¼ fresh thyme, chopped

⅛ tsp. kosher salt and pepper, or more to taste

Small amount of beef or chicken broth

⅞ cup beef or chicken consommé soup

Chervil or parsley, for garnish

Oyster Poche (Poached Oyster) with Ponzu Gelee

SERVES 2

RECIPE BY
MOTOKO HAYASHI

Oyster poche with ponzu gelee is a beautiful and elegant appetizer that is sure to impress your dinner guests.

1   Make the ponzu gelee. In a small pan, mix 6½ Tbsp. of water, soy sauce, rice vinegar, mirin, and sugar and bring it to boil. Remove from heat and add the remaining water and gelatin. Mix well until the gelatin is fully dissolved. Put the mixture in a container and chill in the fridge until it is set.

2   Preheat the water bath to 118°F (48°C).

3   Shuck the oysters, removing each oyster from its shell. Seal the oysters in a plastic bag using the immersion method or a vacuum sealer, ensuring that the oysters form a single layer. Submerge the bag in the water bath. Cook for 30 minutes.

4   Remove the bag from the water bath and place it in an ice bath to stop the cooking process.

5   Discard the oyster liquid from the bag. Crumble the gelee with a fork and serve with the oyster.

9½ Tbsp. water, divided

2⅓ Tbsp. soy sauce

1⅔ Tbsp. rice vinegar

2 Tbsp. mirin (Japanese cooking wine)

1 tsp. granulated sugar

1⅓ tsp. gelatin powder

12 large fresh oysters (Pacific oysters)

Salt to taste

Pork Belly Sliders

SERVES 4

Sliders are a fun party finger food, and pork belly adds a tasty flavor twist. This tough cut needs to be cooked long and slow to make it succulent. In this recipe, we sous vide pork belly for 24–48 hours, then pair it with slaw to make delicious sliders.

1 Preheat the water bath to 149°F (65°C).

2 Seal the pork in a plastic bag using the immersion method or a vacuum sealer. Submerge the bag in the water bath and cook for 24–48 hours.

3 An hour before the pork finishes cooking, prepare the slaw. Mix cabbage, carrots, mayonnaise, Miracle Whip, salt, and pepper.

4 Remove the pork from the bath, pat dry, and sear. Shred the meat and mix it with the Dijon honey mustard.

5 Arrange pork belly and slaw on slider buns, and serve.

1 lb. pork belly

½ head cabbage, cut into thin long strips

1 carrot, cut into thin long strips

3 Tbsp. mayonnaise

1 Tbsp. Miracle Whip

½ tsp. finely ground sea salt

½ tsp. black pepper

2 Tbsp. Dijon honey mustard

1 package slider buns

Ribeye Steak Nachos

SERVES 2

Take your game-day nachos to the next level by adding sous vide ribeye steak.

1 Preheat your water bath to 129°F (53°C).

2 Seal the steak in a plastic bag using the immersion method or a vacuum sealer. Submerge the bag in the water bath and cook for 1 hour.

3 Remove meat from bath, pat dry, and sear on both sides. Slice steak into bite-size pieces and season with salt.

4 To serve, spread chips evenly on a baking sheet and top with steak and cheese. Garnish with chopped scallion and cilantro. Place baking sheet under broiler until cheese is melted. Top with lime juice, sprinkle with extra cilantro and enjoy!

1 lb. ribeye steak

1 tsp. sea salt

1 bag tortilla chips

6 oz. Monterey Jack cheese, shredded

1 scallion, finely chopped

3 sprigs cilantro, finely chopped, plus more for garnish

½ lime, juiced

Sea Scallop Tartare

SERVES 4

RECIPE BY
GEOFFREY BARKER

Sea scallop tartare with smashed avocado, sous vide yolk, and red wine vinegar glaze, garnished with fresh parsley makes a succulent appetizer any night of the week.

SEA SCALLOP TARTARE

1 Preheat the water bath to 135.3°F (57.4°C).

2 Add eggs and cook for 45–60 minutes.

3 Combine scallop meat, onion, mint, basil, chili, and lime juice in a bowl with a generous splash of oil. Mix well and refrigerate for 45 minutes.

4 Dress the serving plate with Red Wine Vinegar Glaze and parsley.

5 Place the smashed avocado on the plate. Drain the excess fluid from the scallop tartare and place it on top of smashed avocado. Separate egg yolks from whites and place on top of tartare.

RED WINE VINEGAR GLAZE

1 Mix red wine vinegar with brown sugar in a saucepan.

2 Bring to a boil and then simmer until reduced by half. Allow to cool prior to use.

SEA SCALLOP TARTARE

4 eggs

1 lb. fresh scallop meat, finely diced

1 red onion, finely diced

24 mint leaves, finely shredded

24 basil leaves, finely shredded

4 red chili, finely sliced

4 limes, juice only

Rice bran oil

Finely chopped parsley, for garnish

2 avocadoes, smashed

RED WINE VINEGAR GLAZE

1 cup red wine vinegar

⅔ cup brown sugar

Stuffed Baby Calamari in Tomato Sauce

RECIPE BY
MOTOKO HAYASHI

SERVES 4

Stuffed baby calamari in tomato sauce makes for a delicious and delicate appetizer or entrée.

1 Preheat the water bath to 145.4°F (63°C).

2 In a small bowl, mix the onion, garlic, rice, calamari legs, oregano, salt, pepper, and 3 Tbsp. of the tomato sauce.

3 Stuff the calamari with the rice mixture.

4 Seal the stuffed calamari and sauce in a plastic bag using the immersion method or a vacuum sealer, ensuring that the calamari form a single layer. Place the bag in the water bath and cook for 20 minutes.

5 To make the sauce, mix the remaining tomato sauce, olives, and capers in a small bowl.

6 Remove the calamari carefully from the bag. Pour the sauce over the calamari. Garnish with parsley and serve.

¼ cup minced onion

1 clove garlic, minced

⅓ cup cooked white rice (use jasmine, Arborio, or Japanese short grain)

⅓ cup calamari legs, chopped

1 tsp. fresh oregano or ½ tsp. dried oregano

⅛ tsp. kosher salt

⅛ tsp. freshly ground pepper

1⅔ cups Sansaire pasta sauce or your favorite tomato sauce, divided

8–12 baby calamari, cleaned

2 Tbsp. sliced black Kalamata olive

2 tsp. capers

Parsley for garnish

Vegan Stuffed Artichoke

RECIPE BY
ZACH ADLEMAN

SERVES 2

Sous vide is hands down the best way that I have ever cooked artichokes. When artichokes are boiled or steamed, so much of their flavor is lost to the water. But by cooking them sous vide, all the flavor is preserved.

1 Cut off stems and pointy ends of artichokes.

2 Preheat the water bath to 185°F (85°C).

3 Seal the artichokes in a plastic bag using the immersion method or a vacuum sealer. Submerge the bag in the water bath and cook 2 hours.

4 Remove from water bath and let cool. Remove inner leaves and furry center of artichokes with a spoon.

5 Sweat onion, celery, and 2 of the garlic cloves for 2 minutes. Add vegan sausage, and let cook for 5 more minutes.

6 Spread the leaves of the artichoke and fill with sausage mixture. Top with panko. Broil until golden brown.

7 Melt vegan butter for dipping. Add remaining garlic, lemon, salt, and pepper to taste. Serve immediately.

2 medium-sized artichokes

½ onion

2 stalks celery

3 garlic cloves

1 (6-oz.) vegan sausage

½ cup panko (breadcrumbs)

½ cup vegan butter

½ lemon

Salt and pepper to taste

Breakfast & Brunch

Asparagus with Sous Vide Egg, Pancetta, and Hollandaise

SERVES 2

When cooked sous vide, asparagus is an incredible treat. We can't think of a better way to celebrate asparagus than by topping it with a sous vide egg, crispy pancetta, and creamy hollandaise sauce.

1 Preheat the water bath to 149°F (65°C). Add eggs in their shells and cook for 45 minutes. Set eggs aside in a bowl of hot tap water to keep them warm until serving, up to 1 hour.

2 Preheat a second water bath to 185°F (85°C).

3 Seal asparagus and butter in a plastic bag using the immersion method or a vacuum sealer. Ensure that the asparagus forms a single layer. Place the bag in the water bath and cook for 15 minutes.

4 Meanwhile, fry the pancetta in a pan until crispy.

5 To serve, divide the asparagus in half, and place each half on a plate. Crack the sous vide eggs over the asparagus. Top with hollandaise sauce, pancetta, lemon zest, cayenne pepper, and salt to taste. Serve immediately.

2 eggs

1 bunch asparagus, trimmed

1 Tbsp. unsalted butter, melted

½ cup pancetta, cubed

¼ cup hollandaise sauce (made ahead, or store bought)

1 tsp. lemon zest

¼ tsp. cayenne pepper

Salt to taste

Bacon and Eggs with Hash Browns

SERVES 4

RECIPE BY
GEOFFREY BARKER

Hot bacon and eggs served over a jalapeño stuffed hash brown, garnished with fresh parsley and chili flakes puts a delightful spin on the traditional bacon and eggs.

1   Preheat the water bath to 145.4°F (63°C).

2   Seal the bacon in a plastic bag using the immersion method or a vacuum sealer, ensuring that the slices form a single layer. Submerge the bag in the water bath and cook for 4–24 hours.

3   One hour before bacon is ready, add 8 eggs to the water bath.

4   Boil the potatoes until tender and mash them. Form the mashed potatoes into 4 hash brown patties and push 4 jalapeno slices into each one.

5   Use the remaining egg to make an egg wash by scrambling the egg with water. Dip each hash brown into the egg wash and panko.

6   Shallow fry hash browns in vegetable oil until golden and crunchy.

7   Remove bacon from sous vide, pat dry, and sear on each side.

8   Place bacon and eggs on top of the hash browns. Garnish with parsley and chili flakes and serve.

16 bacon slices

9 eggs

4 potatoes, peeled and diced

16 pickled jalapeño slices

1 Tbsp. water

Panko (breadcrumbs)

Vegetable oil

Freshly chopped parsley for garnish

Dried chili flakes for garnish

Banana Nut Oatmeal

Eat breakfast on the go! Sous vide banana nut oatmeal is delicious, nutritious, and no fuss in the morning.

1 Preheat the water bath to 154.4°F (68°C).

2 Combine banana with rolled oats, milk, water, cinnamon, and brown sugar or maple syrup to taste.

3 Add the oat mixture to a canning jar (size of your choice), being careful not to fill jar more than ¾ full to allow for expansion.

4 Seal the jar but do not tighten completely. The ring should be slightly loose to allow air to escape. Add to the water bath, ensuring the water level covers the jar. Cook overnight.

5 Add additional sliced bananas and sprinkle with your favorite nuts before serving.

1 banana, smashed, plus more for garnish

⅔ cup of rolled oats

⅔ cup of milk

½ cup water

½ tsp. cinnamon

Brown sugar to taste (optional)

Maple syrup to taste (optional)

1 canning jar

2 Tbsp. walnuts

Breakfast Mushi-Pan (Savory Steamed Muffins)

RECIPE BY
MOTOKO HAYASHI

SERVES 4–5

For a healthy breakfast treat, try mushi-pan or savory steamed muffins. Unlike regular muffins, sous vide keeps them fluffy and moist without becoming too dry. Breakfast mushi-pan can be made with any meat, vegetables, and cheese of your choice such as bacon, sausage, corn, broccoli, or asparagus.

1 Preheat the water bath to 195°F (90.5°C).

2 In a small bowl, sift the flour, baking powder, sugar, and salt. Mix well.

3 Beat 1 egg and add milk. Ensure the mixture measures 10 Tbsp. in total.

4 Add the egg mixture to the flour mixture and mix well.

5 Add the oil into the batter. Mix until everything is combined well.

6 Add the vegetables, ham, and cheese into the batter.

7 Coat the inside of each jar with the vegetable oil. Divide the batter between the prepared jars. Each jar should be no more than half full. Wipe off sides and tops of jars if there are any drips. Firmly tap jars on the counter to remove air bubbles.

8 Seal the jars but do not tighten completely. The rings should be slightly loose to allow air to escape. Add them to the water bath, ensuring the water level covers the jars. Cook for a minimum 2 hours, maximum 3 hours.

9 Remove the jars from the water bath and transfer to a cooling rack. Carefully remove the lids. Cool the muffins for 5 minutes before taking them out of the jars. Run a knife around the sides of the jars if they are hard to take out. Serve hot.

- 1⅔ cups cake flour
- 1½ tsp. baking powder
- 1⅔ Tbsp. granulated sugar
- ¼ tsp. kosher salt, or to taste
- 1 egg
- 7 Tbsp. milk
- 3 Tbsp. canola or vegetable oil, plus more to coat jars
- ¼ cup roasted red bell peppers, cut into bite-size pieces
- ¼ cup roasted yellow bell peppers, cut into bite-size pieces
- 3 Tbsp. green peas, thawed
- 4 slices sandwich ham, cut into bite-size pieces
- 6½ Tbsp. grated white cheddar cheese
- 4–5 (8-oz.) canning jars

Brioche Pain Perdu Jarred with Orange-Infused Maple Syrup

SERVES 4

Brioche pain perdu jarred puts a twist on traditional French toast. Cook in jars for a simple and delicious breakfast treat. Orange-infused maple syrup is simple yet flavorful, making it the perfect topping for pancakes, French toast, or your favorite dish of choice.

BRIOCHE PAIN PERDU JARRED

1   Preheat the water bath to 170.6°F (77°C).

2   In a small bowl, combine cinnamon, nutmeg, and sugar. Whisk in the eggs, milk, vanilla extract, and orange zest. Pour the mixture into a shallow container.

3   Dip the bread in the egg mixture. Soak each side of the bread for 5 minutes.

4   Coat the inside of the jars with butter.

5   Place 1 slice of bread in each jar, divide the excess egg mixture into each jar, then place a second slice in the jar.

6   Seal the jars but do not tighten completely. The rings should be slightly loose to allow air to escape. Add the jars to the water bath, ensuring the water level covers the jars. Cook for 45 minutes.

7   Remove the bread from each jar. In a frying pan, melt the butter and fry each side until golden brown.

8   Serve with the mascarpone cheese and orange-infused maple syrup.

ORANGE INFUSED MAPLE SYRUP

1   Preheat the bath to 135°F (57°C).

2   Seal all of the ingredients in a plastic bag using the immersion method or a vacuum sealer. Submerge the bag in the water bath. Cook for 1–2 hours.

3   Remove the bag from the water bath and submerge it in an ice water bath for 30 minutes.

4   Strain the syrup into a clean bottle and tightly cap. Store in refrigerator for up 2 weeks.

RECIPE BY
MOTOKO HAYASHI

BRIOCHE PAIN PERDU JARRED

½ tsp. ground cinnamon

¼ tsp. ground nutmeg

2 Tbsp. granulated sugar

4 eggs, lightly beaten

1 cup milk

1 tsp. vanilla extract

1 Tbsp. orange zest

8 slices brioche or challah, cut in round pieces 3 inches in diameter and 1-inch thick

4 (16-oz.) canning jars

4 Tbsp. unsalted butter, plus more for coating the jars

3 oz. mascarpone cheese for garnish

ORANGE-INFUSED MAPLE SYRUP
(Yields 2 cups)

2 cups pure maple syrup

Orange rind from 1 orange, beaten with a wooden spoon

Zest from 1 orange

1 cinnamon stick

¼ tsp. fine sea salt

Cheese Mushi-Pan (Cheese Steamed Muffins)

RECIPE BY
MOTOKO HAYASHI

MAKES 4–5

Jump start your day with these savory cheese steamed muffins. These fluffy, moist sous vide muffins make for a healthy and hearty breakfast.

1 Preheat the water bath to 195°F (90.5°C).

2 In a bowl, sift the flour and baking powder.

3 In separate bowl, whisk the cream cheese and sugar.

4 Gradually add eggs into the cream cheese mixture and mix well.

5 Add milk and oil to the cream cheese mixture. Mix well.

6 Add the flour mixture and stir until fully incorporated.

7 Coat the inside of each jar with vegetable oil. Divide the batter between the prepared jars. Each jar should be no more than half full. Wipe off sides and tops of jars if there are any drips. Firmly tap jars on the counter to remove air bubbles.

8 Seal the jars but do not tighten completely. The rings should be slightly loose to allow air to escape. Add them to the water bath, ensuring the water level covers the jars. Cook for a minimum 2 hours, maximum 3 hours.

9 Remove the jars from the water bath and transfer to a cooling rack. Carefully remove the lids. Cool the muffins for 5 minutes before taking them out of the jars. Run a knife around the sides of the jars if they're hard to take out. Serve hot.

1 cup cake flour

1½ tsp. baking powder

6½ Tbsp. cream cheese, at room temperature

⅓ cup granulated sugar

2 eggs, lightly beaten

¼ cup whole milk or low-fat milk

¼ cup canola or vegetable oil, plus more to coat jars

4–5 (8-oz.) canning jars

Chicken-Fried Steak with Maple Bourbon Brown Gravy

RECIPE BY
ZACH ADLEMAN

SERVES 2

The reason why this dish works so well with sous vide is that you can buy an inexpensive cut of meat without having to pound it out. The cooking process tenderizes it for you, and your only remaining challenge is to make sure the crust comes out golden brown.

1 Divide top round into 2 thinly sliced filets.

2 Preheat the water bath to 131°F (55°C).

3 Seal steaks in a plastic bag using the immersion method or a vacuum sealer, ensuring that the meat forms a single layer. Submerge the bag in the water bath and cook for 8 hours.

4 Remove steaks. While they cool, heat the water bath to 161.6°F (72°C). Add 2 eggs to the water bath and cook for 45 min. Remove eggs from bath and set aside.

5 Combine 2 remaining eggs, buttermilk, cayenne, paprika, garlic powder, and onion powder in a bowl to form the batter. Place flour into separate bowl.

6 Coat each steak in flour, then submerge in batter until evenly covered, and return to the bowl of flour to coat again.

7 Fry each steak in vegetable oil until golden brown on both sides. Remove steaks and let rest on a plate lined with paper towels.

8 To make the gravy, add the onion and garlic to fry pan, and cook for 1 minute. Remove from heat, and add bourbon to the pan. Let cook for 1 minute. Return to heat, adding maple syrup and beef stock. Allow sauce to thicken. Add salt and pepper to taste.

9 Serve steak topped with gravy and sous vide eggs.

½ lb. top round sirloin

4 eggs, divided

1 cup buttermilk

½ tsp. cayenne

½ tsp. paprika

1 tsp. garlic powder

1 tsp. onion powder

2 cups flour

½ cup vegetable oil

½ onion, chopped

4 cloves garlic, minced

1½ oz. bourbon

1 Tbsp. maple syrup

1 (14.5 oz.) can beef stock

Salt and pepper to taste

Eggs Benedict

SERVES 2

Sous vide makes perfect medium-poached eggs for a classic eggs Benedict. Whereas poaching an egg is a difficult and noteworthy achievement in traditional cooking, you can perfectly poach eggs sous vide with your eyes closed. By allowing the eggs to cook slowly over 45 minutes, their texture will become fudgy and silken. You're about to upgrade your brunch game.

1 Preheat the water bath to 154.4°F (68°C).

2 Place eggs in sous vide bath and cook for 45 minutes.

3 Make hollandaise sauce 15 minutes before eggs are done. Beat egg yolks, lemon juice, cayenne pepper, water, and Sansaire Steak Aging Sauce until well combined. Pour into a sauce pan over low heat and whisk continuously for 3 minutes, taking pan off the burner periodically. Add butter slowly over the 3 minutes while continuing to whisk, again taking pan off the burner periodically. Remove from heat and cover to keep warm.

4 To serve, butter each slice of the English muffin and add 2 slices browned Canadian bacon. Remove eggs from bath, and gently crack egg over the bacon. Drizzle with hollandaise sauce and garnish with parsley or chives.

2 eggs

2 egg yolks

2 Tbsp. lemon juice

¼ tsp. cayenne pepper

½ Tbsp. water

⅛ tsp. Sansaire Steak Aging Sauce

⅓ cup butter, melted, plus 1 tsp. to spread on the muffin

1 English muffin, toasted

4 strips Canadian bacon, cooked

Italian parsley or chives for garnish (optional)

Eggy Mash Jar

SERVES 4

RECIPE BY
MOTOKO HAYASHI

Sous vide egg mash in jars makes for a simple meal to take on the go.

1   Preheat the water bath to 147°F (64°C).

2   Put ⅓ cup of potato mash (see page 146 for recipe) in each jar and flatten the surface. Crack 1 egg in each jar on top of the potato mash.

3   Seal the jars but do not tighten completely. The rings should be slightly loose to allow air to escape. Add them to the water bath, ensuring the water level covers the jars. Cook for 65 minutes.

4   Remove jars from the water, open the lids, and garnish with a sprinkle of Parmesan cheese, chives, and sea salt.

5   Mix the eggs and potatoes with the salt and chives and enjoy with toasted bread.

1⅓ cup potato mash

4 eggs

4 (8-oz.) canning jars

1 Tbsp. shaved Parmesan cheese

2 Tbsp. chopped chives, plus more for garnish

Pinch of sea salt

Toasted baguette, thinly sliced

Fried Egg Yolks

SERVES 3

Dress up your breakfast with these delicious, fried sous vide eggs.

1   Preheat water bath to 145°F (63°C).

2   Place 3 eggs in water bath and cook for one hour.

3   Remove eggs and let cool in an ice bath.

4   Gently crack eggs and separate out the yolk. Note: The white of the egg will be runny but the yolk will be mostly solid. Some white may cling to the yolk, but it can be carefully removed without damaging the egg.

5   Coat each yolk in flour first, then in the whisked egg, then in panko, and Parmesan cheese.

6   Fry in butter until both sides are lightly brown and crispy or deep fry at 374°F for 30 seconds. Season to taste with salt and pepper.

3 large eggs

1 cup flour

1 egg, whisked

1 cup panko (bread crumbs)

1 Tbsp. Parmesan cheese

4 Tbsp. butter

Salt and pepper to taste

Matcha Mushi-Pan (Green Tea Steamed Muffins)

RECIPE BY
MOTOKO HAYASHI

SERVES 4-5

For a surprising treat, try our sous vide matcha green tea muffins. With all the health benefits of green tea yet a delicious and sophisticated flavor, these muffins will allow you to indulge guilt-free. You can substitute macha green tea powder with cocoa powder.

1 Preheat the water bath to 195°F (90.5°C).

2 In a medium bowl, sift the cake flour, matcha green tea powder, and baking powder together.

3 In a small bowl, mix the eggs, milk, sugar, and oil.

4 Combine egg mixture and flour mixture. Stir well.

5 Coat the inside of each jar with vegetable oil. Divide the batter between the prepared jars. Each jar should be no more than half full. Wipe off sides and tops of jars if there are any drips. Firmly tap jars on the counter to remove air bubbles.

6 Seal the jars but do not tighten completely. The rings should be slightly loose to allow air to escape. Add them to the water bath, ensuring the water level covers the jar. Cook for a minimum 2 hours, maximum 3 hours.

7 When the muffins are done, remove the jars from the water bath and transfer to a cooling rack. Carefully remove the lids. Cool the muffins for 5 minutes before taking them out. Run a knife around the sides of the jars if they're hard to take out. Serve hot, or allow to cool and serve with whipped cream.

1 cup cake flour

2⅔ tsp. matcha green tea powder

2⅔ tsp. baking powder

2 eggs, lightly beaten

9 Tbsp. whole milk or low-fat milk

¼ cup granulated sugar

¼ cup canola or vegetable oil, plus more to coat jars

4–5 (8-oz.) canning jars

Heavy whipped cream, for garnish (optional)

Mushroom and Ham Flan

SERVES 4

RECIPE BY
MOTOKO HAYASHI

This light, savory mushroom and ham egg custard can be served hot or cold, making it perfect for a late morning meal any time of the year. For a twist, try substituting bacon bits for ham.

1 Preheat the water bath to 176°F (80°C).

2 In a small bowl, combine the chicken broth, milk, salt, and pepper.

3 In a separate bowl, beat the eggs. Add broth mixture and strain to achieve a smooth texture.

4 In the bottom of each jar, place ham, shimeji mushrooms, and enoki mushrooms. Divide the egg mixture in four and slowly pour it in each jar.

5 Seal the jars but do not tighten completely. The ring should be slightly loose to allow air to escape. Add them to the water bath, ensuring the water level covers the jar. Cook for 1 hour.

6 Garnish with a celery leaf and thyme.

13 Tbsp. chicken broth

6½ Tbsp. whole milk

½ tsp. salt

Black pepper to taste

2 eggs

4 (8-oz.) canning jars

2 slices ham, diced

1 cup shimeji mushrooms

½ cup enoki mushrooms, cut into 1-inch pieces

Celery leaves for garnish

Fresh thyme for garnish

Scotch Eggs

SERVES 4

RECIPE BY
ZACH ADLEMAN

Although traditionally made with breakfast sausage, this dish can be made with any type of ground meat. Change it up whenever you feel like trying something new.

6 eggs

1 cup flour

1 cup panko
  (breadcrumbs)

12 oz. ground sausage

Vegetable oil

Salt and pepper to taste

1 Preheat the water bath to 165.2°F (74°C).

2 Add 4 eggs to the water bath and cook for 45 minutes.

3 Meanwhile, place the flour, panko, and remaining eggs into separate bowls.

4 Whisk the eggs together until uniform.

5 Remove eggs from sous vide, let cool, and peel.

6 Wrap each sous vide egg in sausage, then roll in flour, the egg mixture, and panko.

7 Fry in a deep-bottomed pot, in 1 inch of vegetable oil until golden brown on all sides.

8 Serve with salt, pepper, and your favorite condiments.

Entrées

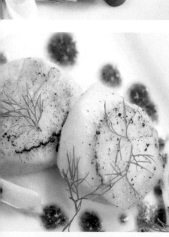

Beef Brisket

SERVES 4–6

RECIPE BY
MOTOKO HAYASHI

This beautiful and delicious beef brisket will make the perfect centerpiece for your dinner table no matter the occasion.

1 Preheat the water bath to 134.6°F (57°C) for medium rare meat.

2 Place the garlic, rosemary, and salt on the cutting board and mince together finely. In a small bowl, mix the rosemary mixture and 1 Tbsp. of the olive oil together.

3 Season the brisket with salt and pepper on both sides, then rub the rosemary and oil mixture on both sides. Sear the meat with the remaining olive oil.

4 Seal the brisket, carrots, celery, onion, red wine, tomatoes, soy sauce, parsley, and bay leaves in a plastic bag using the immersion method or a vacuum sealer. Submerge the bag in the water bath and cook for 48–72 hours. Cover the water surface with a plastic wrap to reduce water evaporation.

5 Remove the brisket and vegetables from the bag. Discard the bay leaves and parsley. Reserve the wine liquid.

6 To make the sauce, bring the wine liquid to a boil in a saucepan. For a thicker sauce, mix 1 Tbsp. of flour into 3 Tbsp. of the wine liquid and add it into the sauce. Reduce by half by boiling for 5–10 minutes. Adjust the seasoning.

7 To serve, cut the brisket against the grain, arrange the vegetables around it, and pour the sauce over the meat.

2 cloves garlic, minced

2 sprigs rosemary, needles stripped from the stem and chopped

½ tsp. kosher salt

2 Tbsp. extra-virgin olive oil, divided

2½ lbs. beef brisket

Kosher salt and ground black pepper for seasoning

2 carrots, cut in 2½–3-inch pieces and halved

1–2 celery stalks, cut in 2½–3 inch pieces

1 onion, cut in 8 wedges

1 cup dry red wine

½ (8-oz.) can whole or diced tomatoes, mashed

1 Tbsp. soy sauce

2 stems fresh flat-leaf parsley leaves

2 bay leaves

1 Tbsp. flour, if you prefer a thicker sauce

Buttermilk Pork Cutlet with Sweet Potato Mash and Greens

RECIPE BY
GEOFFREY BARKER

SERVES 4

This buttermilk pork cutlet entrée served with creamy sweet potato mash and short-cooked greens and topped with applesauce is a great way to incorporate vegetables into your meal with no hassle.

1   Make buttermilk by mixing 2 cups of milk and the vinegar together. Allow the mixture to sit for 15 minutes at room temperature until curdling has commenced.

2   Add pork loin cutlets to buttermilk, cover, and refrigerate for 24–48 hours.

3   Preheat the water bath to 136.4°F (58°C).

4   Remove pork from buttermilk, lightly pat dry, and seal pork in a plastic bag using the immersion method or a vacuum sealer, ensuring that the cutlets form a single layer. Submerge the bag in the water bath and cook for 1 hour.

5   About 20 minutes before pork is ready, bring 4 cups of lightly salted water to boil in a pot and cook sweet potatoes until they are fork-tender, or approximately 10 minutes. Drain sweet potatoes and allow to cool. In the same pot or in another one, bring 4 cups of lightly salted water to boil, cook vegetables for 1 minute, then drain.

6   Place pot back on stove over low heat and add butter and remaining milk, stirring to combine. Add sweet potatoes and mash.

7   Remove pork loin cutlets, pat dry, and sear on both sides.

8   Serve pork and vegetables with a generous splash of applesauce on the side. Enjoy!

2¼ cups milk, divided

2 Tbsp. apple cider vinegar

4 pork loin cutlets

8 cups water, divided

Salt to taste

1 lb. sweet potatoes, peeled and diced

1 cup green beans

½ cup fresh peas

2 Tbsp. butter

Applesauce

Calamari and Octopus Mediterranean Couscous

RECIPE BY
GEOFFREY BARKER

SERVES 4

Sous vide calamari and octopus, tossed with a Mediterranean-spiced pearl couscous, makes for an enjoyable seafood appetizer or entrée.

1   Preheat the water bath to 133.5°F (56.4°C).

2   Seal the calamari and octopus in a plastic bag using the immersion method or a vacuum sealer, ensuring that they form a single layer. Submerge the bag in the water bath and cook for 1 hour.

3   About 20 minutes before calamari and octopus are ready, heat a large saucepan over medium heat, add oil and onion, and sauté for 5 minutes. Add garlic, cumin, coriander, and cinnamon. Continue to cook for 1 minute or until fragrant. Add couscous and cook for 3 minutes. Add wine and cook until absorbed.

4   Add olives, cherry tomatoes, and stock. Bring to a boil, then cover and simmer for 10 minutes.

5   Remove calamari and octopus from water bath and pat dry. Slice calamari into triangles. Add calamari and octopus to couscous and cook for 1 minute.

6   Remove from heat, add mint leaves, and season with salt and pepper to taste.

1 lb. calamari tubes, sliced open and scored in a crisscross pattern

1 lb. baby octopus

Olive oil for sautéing

1 Spanish onion, finely diced

1 garlic clove, crushed

1 Tbsp. ground cumin

1 Tbsp. ground coriander

½ Tbsp. ground cinnamon

1½ cups pearl couscous

¼ cup dry white wine

½ cup seeded Sicilian green olives, halved

½ cup cherry tomatoes, halved

2 cups vegetable stock, boiling

25 mint leaves, finely shredded

Salt and pepper to taste

Chicken Burger

SERVES 2

With Sansaire, you can achieve tender, juicy chicken every time—perfect for making these classic chicken burgers.

1   Preheat the water bath to 155°F (68°C).

2   Season chicken breast with salt and then seal it in a plastic bag using the immersion method or a vacuum sealer, ensuring that the chicken forms a single layer. Submerge the bag in the water bath and cook for at least 1 hour.

3   Remove chicken from water bath, pat dry, and sear on both sides.

4   Place cheese on chicken breast and lightly sear until melted.

5   Top each bun with chicken, lettuce, tomato, and Japanese mayonnaise.

1 whole chicken breast

Salt to taste

2 slices of cheddar cheese

2 potato buns

Lettuce leaves

½ tomato, cut into slices

2 tsp. Japanese mayonnaise

Chicken Wraps

SERVES 2

Sous vide chicken wraps are both hearty and delicious, making for an easy lunch on the go.

1   Preheat the water bath to 155°F (68°C).

2   Seal the chicken and Sansaire Steak Aging Sauce in a plastic bag using the immersion method or a vacuum sealer, ensuring that the chicken forms a single layer. Submerge the bag in the water bath and cook for at least 1 hour.

3   Remove chicken from water bath, pat dry, and sear on both sides. Dice chicken into bite-size pieces and season to taste with salt and onion powder.

4   Lightly sear tortilla and fill with chicken, bell pepper, lettuce, and cheese.

5   Fold the edges of the tortilla toward the center and carefully roll from the bottom until the wrap is fully closed. Enjoy with favorite dipping sauce or salad dressing.

½ lb. chicken breast

½ Tbsp. Sansaire Steak Aging Sauce

Salt to taste

Onion powder to taste, or approximately ½ tsp.

1 flour tortilla

¼ bell pepper, cut into strips

Shredded lettuce

2 Tbsp. shredded cheese

Chilean Sea Bass

Chilean sea bass is a flavorful, flakey white fish. We use a minimalist recipe to preserve the naturally delicate flavor of the fish. Because fish is so delicate, small differences in cooking temperature have a big impact on the final texture. Good thing we leave nothing to chance with Sous Vide.

1 Preheat the water bath to 112°F (50°C).

2 Seal olive oil and sea bass in a plastic bag using the immersion method or a vacuum sealer. Submerge the bag in the water bath and cook for 30 minutes.

3 Remove the fillets from the water bath and pat dry.

4 Season with flaky sea salt and black pepper to taste and serve.

1 Tbsp. olive oil

12 oz. Chilean sea bass fillets, approximately 1-inch thick

Sea salt flakes to taste

Black pepper to taste

Coffee Pork Chops

SERVES 4

RECIPE BY
MOTOKO HAYASHI

Sous vide coffee pork chops are sure to please any coffee lover.

1   Preheat the water bath to 140°F (60°C).

2   In a bowl, combine all of the ingredients except for the pork.

3   Seal the pork and liquid mixture in a plastic bag using the immersion method or a vacuum sealer. Submerge the bag in the water bath and cook for 2–3 hours.

4   Remove the pork from the bag. Remove the thyme stems and reserve the liquid.

5   In a saucepan, boil the liquid over medium heat for 10–15 minutes, or until reduced by half. Adjust the seasoning.

6   Preheat a grill pan and sear the pork on both sides. Serve with the sauce.

1 cup espresso or strong, dark-roasted brewed coffee, cooled

½ cup brown sugar

2 Tbsp. balsamic vinegar

1 Tbsp. Dijon mustard

½ tsp. ground ginger

½ tsp. minced garlic

2 Tbsp. ground onion

Salt and pepper to taste

6–8 sprigs fresh thyme

4 pork chops, 1-inch thick

Cornish Game Hens

SERVES 4

Cornish game hens are a nice change from more common chicken and turkey dishes. They are flavorful and make a lovely single serving poultry dish.

4 Cornish game hens

Olive oil

Salt and black pepper to taste

1 tsp. dried basil

Fresh rosemary sprigs

2 cloves garlic, sliced thin

1   Preheat the water bath to 145°F (65°C).

2   Rub each hen with olive oil, then season lightly with salt, black pepper, and dried basil. Add fresh rosemary and sliced garlic to the hen cavities.

3   Seal each hen in a bag using the immersion method or a vacuum sealer. Submerge the bag in the water bath and cook for a minimum 3 hours, maximum 8 hours.

4   Remove the hens from the water bath, pat dry with a paper towel, and sear on all sides.

5   Serve with your favorite seasonal vegetables. In this photo, we paired Cornish hens with sous vide yams. Enjoy!

Fried Jasmine Rice

SERVES 4

RECIPE BY
MOTOKO HAYASHI

Always a crowd-pleasing favorite, try our sous vide fried jasmine rice. For a vegetarian option, substitute tofu for fried chicken.

1   Preheat the water bath to 186.8°F (86°C).

2   Seal the rice and water in a plastic bag using the immersion method or a vacuum sealer. Submerge the bag in the water bath.

3   In another bag, seal the carrots and onions in a plastic bag using the immersion method or a vacuum sealer. Submerge the bag in the same water bath. Cook the rice and vegetables for 35 minutes.

4   Remove both bags from the bath. Add cold water to the bath and cool the temperature to 62°C. Seal the chicken in a plastic bag using the immersion method or a vacuum sealer. Submerge the bag in the water bath. Cook for at least 60 minutes.

5   Discard the liquid from the vegetable and chicken bags.

6   In a wok/frying pan, heat the vegetable oil and add garlic and ginger. Add the vegetables, chicken, stock, rice, and green peas in the pan. Season with the sake, soy sauce, and mirin. Stir quickly.

7   Add the sesame oil. Mix well.

8   Push the rice to one side of the pan, and add the eggs to the other side. Scramble the eggs, then mix with the rice. Stir well.

9   Garnish with the sesame seeds and chives.

2 cups jasmine rice, rinsed

2½ cups water

1 carrots, diced in ½-inch pieces

½ onions, diced in ½-inch pieces

1 cup chicken breast or firm tofu, diced in ½-inch pieces

2 tsp. vegetable oil

½ tsp. garlic, minced

½ tsp. ginger, minced

2 Tbsp. chicken stock or vegetable stock

½ cup frozen green peas, thawed

1 Tbsp. Japanese sake

1 Tbsp. soy sauce

1 Tbsp. mirin (Japanese cooking wine)

2 tsp. sesame oil

2 eggs, lightly beaten

White sesame seeds, roasted for garnish

Chives/green onions, minced for garnish

Hamburger

SERVES 4

Tired of dried-out grilled burgers? For thick, juicy, restaurant-quality burgers, add Sansaire Steak Aging Sauce and sous vide then sear to perfection with the Sansaire Searing Kit.

1   Preheat water bath to 135°F (57°C).

2   In a large bowl, combine ground beef, garlic, Sansaire Steak Aging Sauce, salt and pepper to taste. Mix thoroughly. Divide the mixture to form 4 patties.

3   Seal patties in a plastic bag using the immersion method or a vacuum sealer. Keep the patties flat and separated. Place bag in the water bath and cook for 1 hour.

4   After the patties are done cooking, take the bag out of the water. Remove the meat from the bag and pat it dry using a paper towel.

5   Sear both sides of the patties using the Sansaire Searing Kit, a hot grill, or a frying pan.

6   Serve on a bun with your favorite toppings.

1 lb. lean ground beef

3 garlic cloves, minced

1 Tbsp. Sansaire Steak Aging Sauce

Salt and pepper to taste

4 hamburger buns

Your favorite hamburger toppings

Homemade Italian Sausage

SERVES 4

A family favorite, this homemade Italian sausage recipe has been passed on for generations. Cooking the sausage in a sous vide bath, then browning it briefly in a cast iron skillet makes it better than ever. Today's sausage grinder/ stuffer kit attachments to stand mixers has made it much easier to make sausage at home.

1 Spread ground pork on cutting board and spread all seasonings on meat.

2 Knead thoroughly until seasoning is blended evenly throughout meat.

3 Put meat in a stainless-steel bowl, cover, and leave overnight in refrigerator.

4 Put meat in casings the next day, using instructions on sausage stuffer.

5 To cook sausages, preheat the water bath to 158°F (70°C).

6 Seal sausages in a plastic bag using the immersion method or a vacuum sealer. Place the bag in the water bath for 1 hour.

7 Take the bag out of the water. Remove sausages from the bag, pat them dry using a paper towel and sear.

1 lb. coarse ground pork butt or loin

1 tsp. salt

½ tsp. black pepper

½ tsp. red hot pepper

½ tsp. fennel seed, crushed in blender

½ tsp. anise seed, crushed in blender

1 garlic clove, minced

1 package sausage casings

Kamo Roast: Japanese-Style Duck Breast

RECIPE BY
MOTOKO HAYASHI

SERVES 4

With Sansaire, achieve perfect medium rare duck every time. This is a versatile dish that can be served warm or cold as an appetizer or a main course.

1   Preheat the water bath to 136.4°F (58°C).

2   Remove the excess fat and score the duck skin against the grain so that the excess fat comes out easily when the meat is seared.

3   In a non stick pan, sear each duck breast skin side down for 2–3 minutes on high heat, or until it is a light golden brown. Flip the breast and sear for another minute or so.

4   Seal the duck breast, soy sauce, mirin, and sake in a plastic bag using the immersion method or a vacuum sealer. Submerge the bag in the water bath. Cook for 90 minutes.

5   Remove breasts from the bag. In a nonstick pan on high heat, sear the duck again, laying it skin side down and applying light pressure until the skin is brown. Ensure that the breasts sear evenly.

6   Cut slices ¼-inch thick and serve with the yuzu kosho.

2 duck breasts

½ cup soy sauce

½ cup mirin (Japanese cooking wine)

½ Japanese sake

Yuzu kosho (Japanese yuzu citrus and green chili pepper paste), as condiment

Lemongrass Tofu Steak

RECIFE BY
MOTOKO HAYASHI

SERVES 2–3

Lemongrass tofu steak is a healthy and delicious alternative to beef steak, and with Sansaire, you can achieve tofu that is tender and flavorful every time.

1 packet extra-firm tofu, cut into 6 slices, ¾-inch thick

2 Tbsp. finely minced lemongrass

½ tsp. finely minced ginger

2 Tbsp. fish sauce

2 Tbsp. brown sugar

½ tsp. red chili pepper flakes

2 Tbsp. vegetable oil, to sear

1   Preheat the water bath to 179.6°F (82°C).

2   Place the tofu slices between a kitchen towel or paper towels for at least 30 minutes to remove the excess water. The more excess water that is removed, the softer the tofu comes out.

3   Mix the lemongrass, ginger, fish sauce, brown sugar, and chili pepper flakes together in a plastic bag.

4   Add the tofu and seal the bag using the immersion method or a vacuum sealer, ensuring the tofu forms a single layer. Place the bag in the water bath for 1 hour.

5   Remove tofu from bag. Heat vegetable oil in a pan on medium heat and sear the tofu on both sides. Sides should be nicely browned and crispy.

6   Serve immediately.

Pollo Poblano with Green Chili Corn

SERVES 4

This recipe showcases the ability of the Sansaire Searing Kit by allowing you to achieve a 360-degree roast on your poblano peppers. Combine the delicious flavor of poblano sauce with perfectly cooked sous vide chicken for a delectable meal. We paired this recipe with our green chili corn.

1   Preheat the water bath to 144°F (62°C).

2   Season chicken with salt and pepper. Seal the chicken with olive oil in a plastic bag using the immersion method or a vacuum sealer, ensuring that the chicken forms a single layer. Submerge the bag in the water bath and cook for 90 minutes.

3   Meanwhile, roast and blacken the poblano peppers using the Sansaire Searing Kit or a broiler. Ensure all sides of the peppers are blackened and the outer skin is cracked. Place roasted peppers in a small bowl and cover with damp paper towel. This will help with the skin removal in the next step.

4   Remove the chicken from the water bath, pat dry, and set aside. To make the poblano sauce, increase the water bath to 185°F (85°C).

5   Scrape the outside of the poblano peppers with a sharp knife. The blackened pepper skin should shed easily; discard the removed skin. Cut off both stems and remove and discard the seeds, then dice the peppers. Combine onion, garlic, chicken stock, cumin, and diced peppers in a plastic bag and seal using the immersion method or a vacuum sealer. Cook for 1 hour. If serving with Green Chili Corn, seal ingredients for that recipe in a separate bag and cook it at the same time and in the same water bath as the poblano sauce.

6   Remove peppers and corn from water bath. Lay corn aside and blend the peppers. Add cilantro and blend until smooth. Season with salt and pepper. Empty the sauce into a small pot and add heavy cream. Bring sauce to a simmer over a stovetop, allowing it to reduce for 10–15 minutes. Remove from heat.

7   Ladle sauce over chicken and serve with corn on the side.

POLLO POBLANO

2 boneless chicken breasts

Salt and pepper to taste

1 Tbsp. olive oil

2 poblano peppers

1 cup minced onion

3 garlic cloves, minced

1 cup chicken stock

1 tsp. ground cumin

¼ cup fresh cilantro

1 cup heavy cream

GREEN CHILI CORN

1 (15-oz.) can of yellow corn, drained

¼ cup diced yellow onion

1 garlic clove, minced

3 Tbsp. diced green chilies

1 tsp. chili powder

1 tsp. ground cumin

1 Tbsp. olive oil

Salt and pepper to taste

Pork Green Chili

RECIPE BY
ZACH ADLEMAN

SERVES 6

This dish is so versatile that you can pair it with almost anything. Put it on your chicken fried steak or over your perfect sous vide eggs.

1   Preheat the water bath to 165.2°F (74°C).

2   Season the pork with salt and pepper, then seal it in a plastic bag using the immersion method or a vacuum sealer, ensuring that the pork forms a single layer. Submerge the bag in the water bath and cook for 24 hours.

3   Meanwhile, torch or broil all peppers until blackened. Remove stems and seeds of peppers.

4   Seal all the vegetables in a plastic bag using the immersion method or a vacuum sealer. Submerge the bag in the water bath and cook for the last hour of the 24-hour cook time.

5   Remove vegetables and pork from water bath. Let the pork cool, then shred it.

6   Blend the vegetables and remaining ingredients until uniform. Then cook in a saucepan at medium heat for 20 minutes. Add shredded pork shoulder and salt and pepper to taste.

7   Serve with sous vide eggs.

3 lb. pork shoulder, cut in 1-inch cubes

Salt and pepper to taste

3 poblano chili peppers

3 jalapeños, chopped

1 onion, chopped

5 cloves garlic, minced

2 cups chicken stock

1 tsp. cumin

1 tsp. oregano

Preserved-Lemon Chicken

SERVES 2

RECIPE BY
MOTOKO HAYASHI

For lemon chicken with a kick, try our sous vide preserved-lemon chicken. Its intense lemon flavor is unlike that of regular chicken, making it a must try.

1   Preheat the water bath to 149°F (65°C).

2   In a small bowl, coat the chicken with sugar, then add the chopped preserved lemon and lemon liquid.

3   Seal the chicken, rosemary, garlic, and wine in a plastic bag using the immersion method or a vacuum sealer. Place the bag in the water bath for at least 2 hours.

4   Remove the chicken from the bag. Heat the oil in a pan and sear the chicken until the surface is browned. Season with salt and pepper. Garnish with preserved lemon wedges, rosemary, and parsley and serve.

2 chicken thighs, with or without skin

2 tsp. sugar

1 wedge preserved lemon, chopped (see page 149 for recipe)

1 tsp. preserved-lemon liquid

1 branch fresh rosemary, more for garnish

1 clove garlic, crushed

3⅓ Tbsp. white dry wine

1 Tbsp. canola or vegetable oil

Salt and pepper to taste

Preserved-lemon wedges, for garnish

Parsley, chopped, for garnish

Rack of Lamb with Sous Vide Infused Mint Butter

SERVES 4

In this recipe, we adopt the classic pairing of lamb and mint by infusing the flavor of fresh mint leaves into butter. To put a perfect, golden crust on the lamb, we briefly deep-fry it after it has been fully cooked sous vide.

LAMB

1 Preheat your water bath to 129°F (54°C). Note: you can cook the mint butter in the same water bath as the lamb.

2 Brush all sides of the meat with soy sauce to season. Seal the rack of lamb in a plastic bag using the immersion method or a vacuum sealer. Submerge the bag in the water bath and cook for a minimum 1 hour, maximum 6 hours.

3 Prepare a narrow pot with tall sides for deep frying. Add enough oil to fill the pot about 2 inches deep and heat to 375°F (190°C) on your stovetop.

4 Remove the rack of lamb from the bag and transfer to a carving board. Pat the meat thoroughly dry with paper towels. With the bone side up, cut the rack of lamb into 2-rib segments. Deep fry the lamb segments, working a few at a time, until a golden crust forms on the outside, about 60 seconds.

5 Garnish with lemon zest, flaky sea salt, Mint Butter, and serve.

MINT BUTTER

1 Preheat your water bath to 129°F (54°C).

2 Seal mint leaves, sugar, and butter in a plastic bag using the immersion method or a vacuum sealer. Submerge the bag in the water bath and cook for a minimum 30 minutes. For a stronger infusion, cook up to 1 hour.

3 Pour the butter mixture through a fine mesh strainer, reserving the strained butter. You may discard the mint leaves. Refrigerate the butter to allow it to harden. Alternatively, place the liquid butter in a metal container within an ice bath and stir the butter until hardened. Reserve butter. Can be made up to 30 days ahead of time and stored covered in the refrigerator, or up to 90 days in the freezer.

LAMB

8 rib rack of lamb, French trimmed

2 tsp. soy sauce

Canola oil, for frying

1 tsp. lemon zest

Flaky sea salt

MINT BUTTER

¾ cup finely chopped mint leaves

1 tsp. sugar

½ cup unsalted butter

Rib Fillet with Potato Gratin, Greens, and Bercy Glaze

SERVES 4

This seared rib fillet served with French potato gratin and short-cooked greens topped with a Bercy glaze can be cooked to your preferred doneness.

1   Preheat the water bath to 131°F (55°C) for a medium rare steak.

2   Seal the steaks in a plastic bag using the immersion method or a vacuum sealer, ensuring that the steaks form a single layer. Submerge the bag in the water bath and cook for 2 hours.

3   Preheat the oven to 356°F (80°C).

4   Melt butter in a fry pan over a low heat and cook onions for 5 minutes.

5   Bring pot of salted water to boil, drop in potatoes and cook for 2 minutes.

6   Butter an 8-inch glass pie plate, layer half the potatoes on the bottom, place onions on top, and layer the remaining potatoes.

7   Beat the eggs and cream together and pour over potatoes and onion. Spread cheese over the top and drizzle with oil. Cook in the oven for 30–40 minutes in the upper third of the oven until top is nicely browned. Allow to sit for 10 minutes prior to cutting.

8   Remove rib fillets, reserve the meat liquid, pat dry, and set aside.

9   Bring a small pot of lightly salted water to a boil. Cook broccoli and green beans for 1 minute, drain well.

10 Make Bercy glaze by heating a fry pan over a medium heat. Sauté shallots for 30 seconds, add white wine, and cook until the sauce thickens. Reduce sauce by half and add reserved meat liquid and butter. Cook for 1–2 minutes. Strain and garnish with spring onion.

11 Sear rib fillets on each side. Plate the rib fillets, potato gratin, and greens, dress with Bercy glaze and garnish with crushed macadamia nuts.

RECIPE BY
GEOFFREY BARKER

4 rib fillet steaks, 1½-inch thick

2 Tbsp. butter, plus more to grease pie plate

2 brown onions, thinly sliced

Water

½ tsp salt, plus more to taste

1 lb. potatoes, peeled and thinly sliced

3 eggs

1½ cups whipping cream

¼ cup grated Swiss cheese

Olive oil

½ head broccoli

¾ cup green beans

1 shallot, chopped

1 Tbsp. white wine

1 tsp. butter

1 stalk spring onion, finely sliced for garnish

1 Tbsp. crushed macadamia nuts

Roast Pork Belly, Vegetables, Sauvignon Mustard Sauce

RECIPE BY
GEOFFREY BARKER

SERVES 4

Sous vide pork belly served with roasted vegetables, short-cooked beans and sauvignon mustard sauce takes about 15 hours to make, but it's worth the wait.

1 Preheat the water bath to 149°F (65°C).

2 Lightly salt the pork, then seal it in a plastic bag using the immersion method or a vacuum sealer, ensuring that the pork forms a single layer. Submerge the bag in the water bath and cook for 15 hours.

3 About 1 hour before pork is ready, preheat the oven to 356°F (180°C).

4 Season potatoes and onions with olive oil, salt, and pepper. Place them in a baking tray with apple pieces and roast in the oven for 1 hour.

5 Remove pork from sous vide, pat dry, and baste skin with malt vinegar and light salt. Place under broiler for 10 minutes or until skin has crisped.

6 Heat a pan over low heat and add butter, mustard, and wine. Slowly cook to create Sauvignon Mustard Sauce. Check seasoning and add salt and/or pepper if required.

7 Bring a small pot of salted water to boil, cook green beans for 1 minute and drain.

8 Plate pork, vegetables, and apple pieces. Spoon sauce on top and enjoy.

2 lbs. pork belly, skin scored

Salt and pepper to taste

8 fingerling potatoes

2 Spanish onions, halved with skin on

2 Tbsp. olive oil

1 apple, cut into 8 pieces

2 Tbsp. malt vinegar

2 Tbsp. butter

1 Tbsp. whole grain mustard

¼ cup sauvignon blanc wine

Water

⅔ cup green beans

Salmon Yuan-Yaki

SERVES 4

RECIPE BY
MOTOKO HAYASHI

Traditionally, salmon has to marinate for a long time before cooking. Use Sansaire to achieve delicious, flavorful salmon yuan-yaki in half the time.

1   Preheat the water bath to 122°F (50°C).

2   Sprinkle salmon with salt and let it sit for 30 minutes. Pat the fish with a paper towel to remove the excess water.

3   Combine Japanese sake, mirin, and soy sauce.

4   Seal the salmon and liquid ingredients in a plastic bag using the immersion method or a vacuum sealer. Submerge the bag in the water bath and cook for 25 minutes.

5   Remove fish from the bag. Heat butter in a pan and sear fish quickly. Serve immediately.

4 pieces of sockeye salmon or any salmon

Salt to taste

½ cup Japanese sake

½ cup mirin (Japanese cooking wine)

½ cup soy sauce

Butter, unsalted

Scallops and Fennel with Yuzu Kosho Sauce

RECIPE BY
MOTOKO HAYASHI

SERVES 4

With sous vide, achieve perfect scallops every time without fear of overcooking. For this recipe, we paired the scallops with Yuzu Kosho, a Japanese yuzu citrus with a spicy green pepper paste over orange-infused fennel.

1 To cook the fennel, preheat the water bath to 185°F (85°C).

2 Seal fennel, orange juice, olive oil, and salt in a plastic bag using the immersion method or a vacuum sealer. Place the bag in the water bath for 20 minutes.

3 Remove fennel from sous vide water bath and discard the liquid. Set aside.

4 To cook the scallops, preheat the water bath to 123°F (51°C).

5 Seal the scallops in a plastic bag using the immersion method or a vacuum sealer. Place the bag in the water bath for 30 minutes.

6 Remove scallops from the water bath, pat dry, and sear with half of the butter.

7 To make Yuzu Kosho Sauce, heat the remaining butter in a saucepan and add Yuzu Kosho.

8 To serve, combine the scallops and fennel on a plate and drizzle the sauce on top. Garnish with fennel leaves.

1 bulb fennel, cut into ¼-inch wedges

1 Tbsp. freshly squeezed orange juice

1 Tbsp. olive oil

Salt to taste

8 large scallops, 1½–2 inches in diameter

4 Tbsp. unsalted butter

2 tsp. Yuzu Kosho

Fennel leaves, for garnish

Sesame Tofu Steak

SERVES 2–3

RECIPE BY
MOTOKO HAYASHI

Sesame tofu steak is a healthy, delicious alternative to beef steak, and with Sansaire, you can achieve tofu that is tender and flavorful every time. Pick your favorite tofu firmness and slice it as thick as you like. The softer and thinner it is, the more flavors the tofu absorbs.

1   Preheat the water bath to 179.6°F (82°C).

2   Place the tofu slices between a kitchen towel or paper towels for at least 30 minutes to remove the excess water. The more excess water that is removed, the softer the tofu comes out.

3   Mix the mirin, soy sauce, and brown sugar together in a plastic bag.

4   Add the tofu to the liquid mixture. Seal the plastic bag using the immersion method or a vacuum sealer, ensuring the tofu forms a single layer. Place the bag in the sous vide bath for 1 hour.

5   After it's done, take out the tofu and sprinkle with flour on both sides.

6   Heat oil in a pan on medium heat. Place the tofu slices on the pan, and sprinkle with half of the sesame seeds. Once that side is nicely browned and crispy, flip slices and sprinkle with the rest of the sesame seeds. Flip once again to brown the sesame seeds. Serve immediately.

1 packet extra firm tofu, sliced into 6 pieces ¾-inch thick

¼ cup mirin (Japanese cooking wine)

2 Tbsp. soy sauce

2 tsp. brown sugar

2 Tbsp. flour

2 Tbsp. sesame oil or vegetable oil

2 Tbsp. roasted white sesame seed

Steak with Wasabi Sauce

RECIPE BY
MOTOKO HAYASHI

SERVES 4

Add a kick to traditional steak with our spicy sous vide wasabi sauce.

1 Preheat the water bath to 125.6°F (52°C).

2 Season the meat with a generous amount of salt and black pepper. Seal the meat, oil, a sprig of thyme, and a bay leaf in a plastic bag using the immersion method or a vacuum sealer. Submerge the bag in the water bath. Cook for 1 hour.

3 Remove the meat, bay leaf, and thyme from the bag and pat the meat dry.

4 Heat a skillet and add half of the butter. Add the remaining bay leaf and a sprig of fresh thyme, then add the meat. Season with salt and pepper if necessary. Sear each side for 2 minutes, then remove meat from the pan and set aside.

5 While resting the meat, make the sauce. Heat soy sauce, mirin, wine, and sugar in the skillet. Bring sauce to a boil, then add wasabi, remaining butter, salt, and pepper. Add more wasabi for a spicier sauce.

6 Serve the meat with the sauce.

2 slices beef ribeye, 1-inch thick

Salt and black pepper to taste

2 Tbsp. extra virgin olive oil

2 sprigs fresh thyme

2 bay leaves

4 Tbsp. butter, as needed

¼ cup soy sauce

¼ cup mirin (Japanese cooking wine)

¼ cup dry red wine

Pinch of sugar

At least 2 tsp. wasabi from tube

Thai Coconut Curry with Tofu

SERVES 4–6

RECIPE BY
MOTOKO HAYASHI

Sous vide Thai coconut curry with tofu pairs perfectly with our jasmine rice. Sansaire helps keep vegetables tender yet crunchy and the tofu flavorful. Sous vide jasmine rice is a great way to make fluffy rice every time! It goes well with curry or use it to make fried rice.

1   Preheat the water bath to 183.2°F (84°C).

2   Place the tofu cubes between a kitchen towel or paper towels for at least 30 minutes to remove the excess water. The more excess water that is removed, the softer the tofu comes out.

3   In a small bowl, whisk the coconut milk, brown sugar, fish sauce, and curry paste together.

4   Seal the tofu, liquid mixture, vegetables, lemongrass, and ginger in a plastic bag using the immersion method or a vacuum sealer, ensuring the tofu forms a single layer. Place the bag in the sous vide bath for 30 minutes.

5   Serve with Jasmine Rice. Garnish with cilantro and lime.

½ packet extra firm tofu, 1-inch cubes

1 can (13.5 fluid oz.) coconut milk

2 Tbsp. brown sugar

1 Tbsp. fish sauce

2 tsp. green Thai curry paste, or more to increase spice

¼ head broccoli, florets only, cut into bite-size pieces

¼ carrot, very thinly sliced

¼ green bell pepper, thinly sliced into 2-inch-long strips

¼ red bell pepper, thinly sliced into 2-inch-long strips

½ onion, thinly sliced

1 stalk lemongrass, hit with rolling pin or head of knife and smashed

3 thin slices fresh ginger root

2 cups cooked Jasmine Rice (See page 145)

Cilantro, for garnish

Lime, for garnish

The 195 Cheeseburger

SERVES 2

RECIPE BY
GEOFFREY BARKER

This 195-hour beef short rib with torched Jarlsberg cheese, bread-and-butter pickles, and seeded mustard on a toasted bun makes a mouthwatering, tender, juicy burger that's sure to impress your taste buds—and your guests, of course.

1   Boil water and add brown sugar and salts, allow to cool. Once cooled, add the 2 beef short ribs and refrigerate for 3–7 days.

2   Remove ribs from brine and pat dry. Mix dry rub ingredients. Coat ribs with dry rub. Smoke ribs for 3 hours at 212°F (100°C) over wood cedar chips.

3   Preheat the water bath to 167°F (75°C).

4   Allow ribs to cool, then seal the ribs in a plastic bag using the immersion method or a vacuum sealer, ensuring that the ribs form a single layer. Submerge the bag in the water bath and cook for 24 hours.

5   Remove ribs, pat dry, and sear on each side. Debone ribs.

6   Lightly toast burger buns. Layer with beef ribs, pickles, seeded mustard, and cheese. Sear cheese. Enjoy with fries.

BRINE

8 cups water

⅔ cup brown sugar

⅔ cup kosher salt

2 tsp. pickling salt (optional)

2 beef short ribs

DRY RUB

1 Tbsp. smoked paprika

½ Tbsp. coriander

½ Tbsp. cumin

1 Tbsp. salt

1 tsp. cayenne pepper

2 Tbsp. brown sugar

BURGERS

Wood cedar chips, for smoking

2 burger buns

Bread-and-butter pickles

Seeded mustard

2 slices Jarlsberg cheese

Turkey Breast

SERVES 4

Roasting a whole turkey is fraught with compromise. Dark meat is best at one temperature, while white meat is best at another. Whole turkeys are heavy and hard to negotiate out of the oven, and in a moment's inattention, they overcook and become dry. Using the Sansaire, you can cook the most flavorful, succulent turkey you've ever tasted.

Boneless turkey breast

3 Tbsp. olive oil

Salt, to taste

1 Preheat the water bath to 140°F (60°C).

2 Seal the turkey breast, olive oil, and salt in a plastic bag using the immersion method or a vacuum sealer. Submerge the bag in the water bath and cook for a minimum 2½ hours, maximum 8 hours.

3 Remove the bag from the water bath. Pat dry the turkey breast with a paper towel and sear using the Sansaire Searing Kit, broiler, or pan.

4 Slice the turkey breast crosswise into medallions and arrange on a platter.

Sides

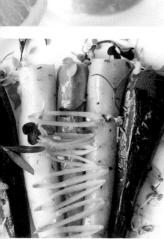

Brussels Sprouts with Bacon and Garlic

SERVES 4

Sous vide brussels sprouts with sautéed bacon and garlic puts a unique twist on a classic side dish.

1   Preheat the water bath to 185°F (85°C).

2   Season brussels sprouts with salt, and then seal in a plastic bag using the immersion method or a vacuum sealer, ensuring that the sprouts form a single layer. Submerge the bag in the water bath and cook for 1½–2 hours.

3   Meanwhile, use oil to sauté the garlic and bacon on medium heat until aromatic.

4   Remove brussels sprouts from sous vide water bath and combine with garlic and bacon mixture.

5   Season with salt, Parmesan cheese, and lemon juice.

1 lb. brussels sprouts

2 tsp. salt, plus more to taste

1 Tbsp. olive oil

2 tsp. garlic, minced

1 lb. bacon

1 tsp. grated Parmesan cheese

2 tsp. lemon juice

Cajun Stuffing

Stuffing is an amazing staple at any holiday dinner table. Here is a Cajun take on this hearty side item. The perfectly cooked sous vide sausage takes this dish up several notches.

1   Preheat the water bath to 150°F (66°C).

2   Seal the sausage in a plastic bag using the immersion method or a vacuum sealer. Submerge the bag in the water bath and cook for 1–4 hours.

3   Fill a small pot of water with water and butter. Bring the pot of water and butter to a boil. Once boiling, add the stuffing mix. Stir until completely mixed and remove from heat. Cover pot and set aside.

4   Add olive oil to a large frying pan on medium heat. Once the oil is hot, add the peppers and onion and sauté for 10 minutes or until softened. When the vegetables are tender, add the minced garlic and Cajun seasoning and continue to cook for 1–2 minutes. Remove from heat and set aside.

5   Remove the sausage from water bath, pat dry, and sear on all sides. Dice the sausage and combine with vegetable mixture in pan.

6   Using a large mixing bowl, combine the stuffing and the vegetable/sausage mix. Mix thoroughly and add salt and pepper to taste as well as more Cajun seasoning as desired.

1½ lb. andouille sausage

1¾ cups water

6 Tbsp. butter

10 oz. stuffing mix

1 Tbsp. olive oil

1 green bell pepper, diced

1 red bell pepper, diced

1 yellow onion, diced

6 cloves garlic, minced

1 Tbsp. Cajun seasoning, plus more to taste

Salt and pepper to taste

Cauliflower and Romanesco with Indian Spices

SERVES 4

RECIPE BY
MOTOKO HAYASHI

Cauliflower and romanesco with Indian spices makes for a simple and delicious side dish. Even when cooked sous vide, the cauliflower and romanesco retain their crunchy texture.

1   Preheat the water bath to 183°F (84°C).

2   In a bowl, toss the cauliflower and romanesco with coriander, cumin, curry powder, turmeric powder, and ginger, and drizzle with about half the olive oil.

3   Seal the seasoned florets in a plastic bag using the immersion method or a vacuum sealer, ensuring that the florets form a single layer. Submerge the bag in the water bath and cook for 45 minutes.

4   Remove the florets from sous vide bath, drain any accumulated liquid. Transfer the florets to a bowl, drizzle with the remaining olive oil, and season with salt and pepper to taste.

5   Toss and garnish with lime zest and cilantro.

½ large head cauliflower, broken into 1-inch florets

½ large head romanesco broccoli, broken into 1-inch florets

½ tsp. coriander seeds

½ tsp. cumin seeds

½ tsp. curry powder

½ tsp. turmeric powder

½ tsp. finely grated, peeled ginger

1 Tbsp. olive oil, divided

Kosher salt and freshly ground black pepper to taste

½ tsp. finely grated lime zest, for garnish

1 Tbsp. freshly minced cilantro leaves, for garnish

Walnut Chili Oil

RECIPE BY
MOTOKO HAYASHI

YIELDS 1 CUP

Walnut chili oil can be used as a condiment on your favorite dish to add just the right amount of spice. It's a great condiment for hamburgers, tacos, grilled beef, tofu, fried rice, miso soup, noodle soup, or any other dishes you want to spice up.

1   Preheat the water bath to 131°F (55°C).

2   Seal all ingredients in a plastic bag using the immersion method or a vacuum sealer. Place the bag in the water bath for at least 3 hours. The longer it cooks, the spicier it will get.

3   Put into a clean, dry container with stopper. The oil will store in the fridge for several months.

2 Tbsp. canola oil

¼ cup roasted sesame oil

¼ cup walnuts, chopped, roasted

2 Tbsp. red chili pepper flakes

3 Tbsp. white sesame seeds, roasted

3 Tbsp. onion, minced

2 cloves garlic, minced

½ tsp. kosher salt

Cranberry Sauce

YIELDS ½ CUP

Sous vide cranberry sauce will make a delicious addition to your holiday table this year.

½ lb. fresh cranberries

1 tangerine

¼ cup sugar

Pinch of salt

1 Preheat water bath to 180°F (82°C).

2 Split all the ingredients in half into 2 plastic bags or jars. If using jars, seal the jars but do not tighten completely. The rings should be slightly loose to allow air to escape. Add them to the water bath, ensuring the water level covers the jar. If using a plastic bag, seal the bag using the immersion method or a vacuum sealer. Submerge the bag in the water bath. Cook for at least 2 hours.

3 Remove bags or jars. Shake vigorously or blend ingredients for a few seconds until it reaches the desired consistency.

Fava Bean and Asparagus Risotto

RECIPE BY
MOTOKO HAYASHI

SERVES 4

Enjoy fresh spring vegetables with this fava bean and asparagus risotto. Fava beans can be substituted with fresh green peas or frozen ones. If you use frozen peas, thaw and warm them up a bit before mixing with rice.

1   Preheat the water bath to 183.2°F (84°C).

2   Heat half of the olive oil and 1 Tbsp. of the butter in a large skillet over low heat. Add the onion and cook, stirring frequently, about 5 minutes. Add the garlic and cook for 1 minute.

3   Stir in the rice and cook for 1 minute. Add white wine. Bring to a rapid simmer and cook until liquid is almost completely evaporated.

4   Seal the rice mixture and broth in a plastic bag using the immersion method or a vacuum sealer. Submerge the bag in the water bath. Cook for 55 minutes.

5   In a separate bag, seal the asparagus, fava beans, and remaining olive oil in a plastic bag using the immersion method or a vacuum sealer, ensuring that the vegetables form a single layer. Submerge the bag in the water bath in the last 15 minutes of the rice cook time.

6   After 55 minutes, check the rice. If it's still firm, cook 5 minutes longer and check every 5 minutes until the rice is soft.

7   Remove the rice and vegetables from the bags and mix all together in a large bowl with the remaining butter, lemon zest, Parmesan cheese, and pepper. Adjust the seasoning.

8   Garnish with grated Parmesan cheese and freshly ground black pepper. Serve immediately.

2 Tbsp. olive oil, divided

3 Tbsp. butter, unsalted, divided

1 cup chopped onion

1 clove garlic, minced

1 cup arborio or carnaroli rice

½ cup dry white wine

2 cups chicken or vegetable broth

½ lb. asparagus, cut 1½ inches in length

½ cup fresh fava beans, removed from the pouch, branched and peeled

1 Tbsp. lemon zest

½ cup grated Parmesan cheese, plus more for garnish

½ tsp. freshly ground black pepper, plus more for garnish

Salt to taste

Infused Oil

Adding flavor to oil is easy with sous vide. Try adding herbs, garlic, or pepper for a distinct taste. Refrigerate and use within 10 days.

1 Preheat the water bath to 131°F (55°C).

2 Add herbs, garlic, and/or pepper to a canning jar or bag.

3 Add oil to the canning jar or bag.

4 If using jars, seal the jars but do not tighten completely. The ring should be slightly loose to allow air to escape. Add them to the water bath, ensuring the water level covers the jar. If using a plastic bag, seal the ingredients in a plastic bag using the immersion method or a vacuum sealer. Submerge the bag in the water bath. Leave in the bath for 3–4 hours.

5 Remove, cool, then refrigerate. Use within 10 days.

Herbs (thyme, rosemary, basil, oregano, other), garlic cloves, or hot peppers

Oil of your choice (olive, canola, grapeseed, or other)

OPTIONS/EXAMPLES
BY MOTOKO HAYASHI

ROSEMARY OIL

½ cup olive oil

3 fresh rosemary sprigs (each 5 inches long)

BASIL OIL

½ cup extra virgin olive oil

1 cup packed basil leaves

MINT OIL

¼ cup extra virgin olive oil

4 sprigs fresh mint (about 30 leaves)

Lemon Black Pepper Infused Oil

RECIPE BY
MOTOKO HAYASHI

YIELDS 1 CUP

Sansaire makes it possible to create your own oils quickly and easily right at home. This lemon black pepper infused oil pairs great with your favorite salad or pasta dish.

2 lemons

½ tsp. kosher salt, plus more to taste

1 cup olive oil

20 black peppercorns, crushed

1   Preheat the water bath to 131°F (55°C).

2   With a vegetable peeler or a citrus zester, remove the zest from the lemons in thin strips. In a mortar or medium stainless steel or wooden bowl, combine the lemon peel and salt. Pound and crush the peel with a pestle for several minutes to extract the oils. Use a circular motion to crush the peel against the bottom of the bowl while dribbling in the olive oil a little at a time. Continue working the peel for about a minute.

3   Seal the lemon oil mixture and 20 peppercorns in a plastic bag using the immersion method or a vacuum sealer. Place the bag in the water bath for 2   3 hours.

4   Add additional olive oil if necessary to balance the flavor. Strain into clean, dry bottles and stopper. The oil will store in the fridge for several months.

Mushroom Risotto

SERVES 4

Sous vide makes this traditional Italian comfort food simple. For a fresh twist on a classic dish, try substituting mushrooms with other vegetables such as peas or asparagus. For a vegetarian option, substitute vegetable stock for chicken stock.

1 Preheat the water bath to 194°F (90°C).

2 Seal the rice and stock in a plastic bag using the immersion method or a vacuum sealer. Submerge the bag in the water bath. Cook for 60 minutes. Halfway through cooking, seal and submerge the mushrooms in separate plastic bag.

3 Remove the rice and mushrooms from the bags, and drain excess liquid. In a bowl, combine together with the cheese, wine, butter, salt, and pepper. Adjust the seasoning.

4 Garnish with grated Parmesan cheese and tomatoes. Serve immediately.

1¾ cups arborio rice

5 cups chicken or vegetable stock at room temperature

1½ cups sliced crimini mushrooms

1 cup freshly grated Parmesan cheese, plus more for garnish

½ cup sauvignon blanc wine

4 Tbsp. unsalted butter, melted

1 tsp. finely ground sea salt

2 tsp. black pepper

Cherry tomatoes, for garnish

Pasta Sauce

YIELDS 6 CUPS

Why sous vide pasta sauce? Cooking on a stove requires oversight and frequent stirring to prevent burning. With sous vide you get the same great taste and the sauce can cook for hours with no oversight. There's pot to clean which is an added benefit.

1   Preheat the water bath to 194°F (90°C).

2   Seal all of the ingredients except the tomato paste and water in a plastic bag using the immersion method or a vacuum sealer. Submerge the bag in the water bath and cook for 15 minutes.

3   Remove the sauce from the water bath. Add the tomato paste and water. Reseal the bag as described in step 2 but this time clip the bag to the top of the pot with one edge slightly unsealed to allow steam to escape. Cook sauce for 3 hours.

4   Remove the bag from the water bath, remove bay leaf, pour sauce into a bowl with pasta and serve. Alternatively, the sauce can be stored for up to 1 week in the refrigerator or 1 month in the freezer.

1 small whole onion, diced

1 tsp. dried oregano

1½ tsp. fresh basil, chopped

2 cloves garlic, chopped

1 whole bay leaf

1 (28-oz.) can crushed tomatoes

1 (18-oz.) can tomato paste

4½ cups water

Pearl Onions with Raisins

SERVES 8

Onion is a nice contrasting flavor to many meals.

1 Preheat the water bath to 185°F (85°C).

2 Seal all the ingredients in a plastic bag using the immersion method or a vacuum sealer. Submerge the bag in the water bath and cook for 1 hour.

3 Remove the bag from the bath and chill quickly by plunging it into a bowl of ice water. Store in the refrigerator until 2 hours before serving. Can be made up to 5 days ahead.

½ tsp. kosher salt

4 Tbsp. butter, cubed

2 Tbsp. red wine vinegar

4 cup pearl or cipollini onions

¼ cup golden raisins

Jasmine Rice

SERVES 6

1 Preheat the water bath to 199.4°F (93°C).

2 Wash and rinse the rice.

3 Seal the rice and water in a plastic bag using the immersion method or a vacuum sealer. Place the bag in the water bath for 35 minutes.

4 Remove the bag. Serve immediately.

2 cups jasmine rice

2 cups water, filtered

Potato Mash

SERVES 4

RECIPE BY
MOTOKO HAYASHI

Sous vide potato mash is a simple and delicious side that pairs perfectly with your favorite entrée.

1   Preheat the water bath to 194°F (90°C).

2   Seal the potatoes, butter, milk, and salt in a plastic bag using the immersion method or a vacuum sealer, ensuring that the potatoes form a single layer. Submerge the bag in the water bath and cook for 30 minutes until the potatoes are tender.

3   Transfer the potatoes to a bowl. Mash with a potato masher or food mill to your desired consistency.

4   Taste and adjust seasonings with salt and pepper to your preference. Top with chives.

1 lb. russet potatoes, peeled and sliced in pieces ½-inch thick

½ cup butter, softened

½ cup whole milk, warmed

¼ tsp. kosher salt, plus more to taste

Pepper to taste

½ cup finely snipped fresh chives, for garnish

Preserved Lemon

RECIPE BY
MOTOKO HAYASHI

YIELDS 1½ CUPS

Preserved lemon is a common condiment in South Asian and North African cuisine. It is traditionally made by packing lemons in salt for one or more months, but a sous vide machine speeds up the process.

1 Preheat the water bath to 183°F (83.9°C).

2 Cut the lemons into quarters. Seal the lemon, salt, bay leaf, black peppercorns, and optional ingredients in a plastic bag using the immersion method or a vacuum sealer. Massage the salt into the lemons, making sure that all the lemons are covered with salt. Place the bag in the water bath for 1 hour.

3 Remove the bag from the water bath and put all ingredients into a clean glass jar with a lid. The lemons will last in the refrigerator for several months.

4–5 organic lemons

Salt, 10% of lemon weight

1 bay leaf

1 tsp. black peppercorns

½ tsp. coriander seeds (optional)

½ tsp. cumin seeds (optional)

Rainbow Carrot Salad

SERVES 4

Carrots come in several vibrant colors in addition to the orange we typically associate with this veggie. Deep purple, bright yellow, and traditional orange add a colorful and flavorful pop to your table.

Cooking vegetables sous vide has a number of advantages over the traditional methods of steaming or boiling. Because the vegetables cook in a sealed bag, they retain all of their nutrients and, more important, all of their flavor. The natural sugars in vegetables are water-soluble, and in a boiling or steaming pot, these sugars are whisked away into the surrounding water, leaving your vegetables dull and bland. When cooked sous vide, however, those flavors stay where they belong. And, as you'd expect, there's no guesswork or fork-probing required to know when your vegetables are properly cooked.

1 lb. rainbow carrots, peeled

1 Tbsp. salt

1 Tbsp. granulated sugar

3 Tbsp. butter

Salt and pepper to taste

Dijon mustard vinaigrette to taste (optional)

*If you aren't using a vacuum sealer, melt the butter before adding it to the other ingredients. Use the immersion method to seal the bag before submerging it in the water bath.

1 Preheat water bath to 183°F (82°C).

2 Separate carrots by color.

3 Combine carrots, salt, sugar, and butter in a bag and seal.*

4 Add bag to water bath and cook for 60 minutes.

5 Remove carrots from bag and arrange on a serving dish. Season to taste with salt and pepper.

6 Drizzle salad with Dijon mustard vinaigrette or your favorite dressing.

Ramen Eggs

SERVES 4

RECIPE BY
MOTOKO HAYASHI

Sous vide ramen eggs have creamy yolks perfect for pairing with ramen and salads, or enjoying as an appetizer.

1 Preheat the water bath to 185°F (85°C).

2 Add eggs to the water bath and cook for 12 minutes.

3 Transfer eggs to a large bowl of ice water to stop the cooking process.

4 Once the eggs are cool, remove them from the ice water, and reheat in boiling water for 2 minutes to cook the egg whites.

5 As soon as the eggs are reheated, transfer them back to the ice water. Once they have cooled, peel off the shells.

6 In a separate bowl, combine soy sauce, mirin, and ketchup. Add the eggs and marinate in the refrigerator for a minimum 2 hours, maximum 6 hours, turning occasionally. The eggs will keep in the refrigerator for up to a month.

7 Serve the eggs on ramen, a salad, or as an appetizer.

4 eggs

⅓ cup soy sauce

4 Tbsp. mirin (Japanese cooking wine)

1 Tbsp. ketchup

Roasted Cipollini Onions with Honey Balsamic Vinegar Sauce

RECIPE BY
MOTOKO HAYASHI

SERVES 4

Roasted cipollini onions with honey balsamic vinegar sauce pairs perfectly with your favorite entrée. It's a sweet and tangy side that goes great with any roast meat dish. For a slightly different flavor, use pearl onions in place of cipollini.

1   Preheat the water bath to 185°F (85°C).

2   Seal the onions, olive oil, water, bay leaves, and lemon zest in a plastic bag using the immersion method or a vacuum sealer. Place the bag in the water bath and cook for 90 minutes.

3   Remove onions from the bath. Reserve the liquid from the bag. Heat olive oil in a pan and sear onions until the surfaces are browned.

4   To make sauce, mix honey, ¼ cup of the liquid from the onion bag, balsamic vinegar, salt, and pepper. Heat in the pan, seasoning with salt and pepper. Heat the sauce until it's thickened.

5   Drizzle the sauce over the onions.

1½ lbs. red or regular cipollini onions, cut in half horizontally*

2 Tbsp. extra virgin olive oil

4 Tbsp. water

2 bay leaves

4 strips of zest from 1 lemon

1 Tbsp. olive oil, for searing

⅓ cup honey

½ cup balsamic vinegar

¼ tsp. kosher salt, plus more to taste

Pepper to taste

*If substituting pearl onions, do not cut —use them whole.

Soups & Salads

Asian Inspired Steak Salad

Add a healthy and delicious spin to your everyday salad with this Asian inspired steak salad.

1 Preheat the water bath to 131°F (55°C).

2 Seal steak in a plastic bag using the immersion method or a vacuum sealer, ensuring that the steak forms a single layer. Submerge the bag in the water bath and cook for at least 1 hour.

3 Meanwhile, prepare dressing by combining lime juice, lemon juice, Sansaire Steak Aging Sauce, and brown sugar. Mix well.

4 Cook soba according to package instructions, and let cool to room temperature.

5 Remove the steak from water bath, drain excess liquid, pat dry, and sear on both sides.

6 Slice steak into thin strips. Combine lettuce, soba and steak strips. Stir in dressing to taste, then garnish with scallions and cilantro.

1 lb. steak

2 Tbsp. lime juice

1 Tbsp. lemon juice

½ tsp. Sansaire Steak Aging Sauce

1 tsp. brown sugar

1 package soba (Japanese buckwheat noodles)

Romaine lettuce, chopped

Scallions, chopped, for garnish

Cilantro, chopped, for garnish

Beet Poke

SERVES 6

RECIPE BY
ZACH ADLEMAN

This is a great substitute for fish, while still getting the sushi restaurant experience. Experiment with this recipe by adding chilies or fruit to the poke.

1 Preheat the water bath to 185°F (85°C).

2 Seal beets in a plastic bag using the immersion method or a vacuum sealer, ensuring that the beets form a single layer. Submerge the bag in the water bath and cook for 1 hour.

3 Remove from water bath, let cool, peel, and dice.

4 Put the beets into a bowl. Toss in remaining ingredients. Marinate for a minimum of 1 hour.

5 Serve over favorite salad or sushi rice.

6 beets of any color

1 Tbsp. rice wine vinegar

1 Tbsp. soy sauce

½ tsp. sesame oil

2 green onions

1 Tbsp. roasted sesame seeds

Chicken Salad

SERVES 4

Sous vide chicken salad provides a sweet and savory take on a lunchtime classic.

1 Preheat water bath to 152°F (66.7°C).

2 Seal the chicken in a plastic bag using the immersion method or a vacuum sealer. Submerge the bag in the water bath and cook for a minimum 1 hour, maximum 6 hours.

3 Remove the chicken from the water bath and pat dry. Sear if desired, and then slice into bite-size pieces. Season with salt and pepper.

4 Combine chopped fruits, veggies, and bacon with chicken in a large mixing bowl. Add mayo and vinaigrette to mixture and stir gently in a folding motion.

5 Cover bowl and refrigerate for 3 hours or until cool. Spoon onto a sourdough roll and enjoy.

1 lb. chicken

1 tsp. salt

½ tsp. black pepper

1 cored apple, chopped into bite-size pieces

10–15 grapes, chopped into bite-size pieces

1 celery stalk, chopped into bite-size pieces

½ small red onion, chopped into bite-size pieces

1 clove garlic, minced

1 scallion, chopped into bite-size pieces

1 colored bell pepper, chopped into bite-size pieces

2 slices cooked bacon, chopped into bite-size pieces

2 Tbsp. mayonnaise

2 Tbsp. champagne vinaigrette

Sourdough sandwich rolls

Chilled Carrot Soup

SERVES 2

Sous vide chilled carrot soup is a refreshing addition to summer meals. Pairs great with grilled cheese sandwiches.

1 Preheat the water bath to 185°F (85°C).

2 Seal all the ingredients except water in a plastic bag using the immersion method or a vacuum sealer. Submerge the bag in the water bath and cook overnight, or approximately 8–10 hours.

3 Pour entire contents of bag into a bowl, add water, and blend, adding up to another cup of water until the soup reaches desired consistency.

4 Top with one of these optional garnishes: crème fraîche, sour cream, chopped parsley, chopped cilantro, chopped chives, croutons and/or sautéed panko. Allow soup to cool and then serve.

1 lb. carrots, peeled and sliced

¼ cup butter, melted

Dash of cayenne pepper

Salt to taste

1 Tbsp. brown sugar

2 Tbsp. orange juice, fresh squeezed

¼ tsp. cinnamon

¼ tsp. paprika

At least 2 cups water

Optional garnishes (see step 4)

crème fraîche

sour cream

chopped parsley

chopped cilantro

chopped chives

croutons and/or sautéed panko

Crispy Skin Duck with Green Mango Salad

RECIPE BY
GEOFFREY BARKER

SERVES 4

Crispy skin duck served over a fresh green mango and pear salad and drizzled with Vietnamese dressing, is perfect for a summer meal.

1   Preheat the water bath to 135.3°F (57.4°C).

2   Seal the duck breast in a plastic bag using the immersion method or a vacuum sealer, ensuring that the duck breasts form a single layer. Submerge the bag in the water bath and cook for 1 hour.

3   Make Vietnamese dressing by combining water, fish sauce, palm sugar, and lime juice. Set aside to cool.

4   Combine the remaining ingredients, excluding parsley, in a bowl. Add dressing and set aside, reserving some chilies and Vietnamese dressing for garnish.

5   Remove duck breasts, pat dry, and sear each side to create crispy skin. Slice each duck breast into 7 pieces.

6   Divide Green Mango Salad between plates. Place each sliced duck breast on top of the plated salad. Drizzle with reserved dressing and garnish with parsley and chilies.

4 duck breasts

VIETNAMESE DRESSING

2 Tbsp. boiling water

2 Tbsp. fish sauce

2 Tbsp. palm sugar, finely grated

2 limes, juiced

GREEN MANGO SALAD

2 green mangoes, julienned

1 carrot, peeled and julienned

1 pear, julienned

1 red bell pepper, thinly sliced

2 red chilies, thinly sliced, plus more for garnish

¼ cup cashews, crushed

Curly leaf parsley, finely chopped for garnish

Lemon Pepper Chicken over Kale Salad

SERVES 2

For a healthy yet delicious take on traditional kale salad, try sous vide lemon pepper chicken with our creamy vinaigrette dressing.

1   Preheat the water bath to 144°F (62°C).

2   Seal the chicken breasts, lemon juice, lemon pepper, and olive oil in a plastic bag using the immersion method or a vacuum sealer, ensuring that the chicken breasts form a single layer. Submerge the bag in the water bath and cook for 90 minutes.

3   Using a fork, combine the garlic, shallot, lemon zest, mayonnaise, and red wine vinegar in a bowl. Optional: drizzle some olive oil into the dressing.

4   Mix dressing into the kale.

5   Remove chicken from the water bath, pat dry, and sear. Cut chicken into ¼-inch strips and season with salt and pepper. Place chicken strips and tomatoes over kale salad and serve immediately.

2 chicken breasts

½ lemon, juiced

1 Tbsp. lemon pepper

¼ cup olive oil

2 cloves garlic, minced

1 Tbsp. minced shallot,

1 tsp. lemon zest

3 Tbsp. mayonnaise

3 Tbsp. red wine vinegar

½ bunch of kale, chopped

Salt and pepper to taste

Cherry tomatoes for garnish

Lobster Salad

SERVES 2

Enjoy a fresh lobster salad sandwich. Sous vide shellfish with Sansaire is easy, consistently tender, and never overcooked.

1   Preheat the water bath to 134°F (56°C).

2   Seal the lobster tails, lemon slices, butter, and parsley in a plastic bag using the immersion method. Submerge the bag in the water bath and cook for 30 minutes (40 minutes, if tails are in their shell).

3   Remove the lobster from the water bath, drain, and let cool. Then shred the lobster meat into a bowl.

4   Add the onion, bell pepper, celery, and mayonnaise to the bowl, mix until combined.

5   Lightly toast brioche bun, fill with lobster salad, and serve.

2 lobster tails

2 lemon slices

2 Tbsp. unsalted butter

A few sprigs of Italian parsley

1 medium red onion, minced

1 red bell pepper, diced

1 celery stalk, diced

¼ cup mayonnaise

Brioche buns

Potato Leek Soup

SERVES 4

Savory sous vide potato leek soup makes for the perfect meal on a cold winter's day.

1 Preheat the water bath to 185°F (85°C).

2 Seal the leeks, potatoes, garlic, thyme, salt, and pepper in a plastic bag using the immersion method or a vacuum sealer. Submerge the bag in the water bath and cook for 1 hour.

3 After the leeks and potatoes are fully cooked, blend with the chicken broth until the soup reaches your desired consistency.

4 Heat the blended ingredients in a pot and add the heavy cream. Let soup simmer for 15–20 minutes, then serve.

2 leeks, chopped (remove dark green)

2 russet potatoes, peeled and cut into ½-inch cubes

3 garlic cloves, minced

1–2 fresh thyme sprigs, chopped

Salt and ground black pepper to taste

4 cups chicken broth

½ cup heavy cream

Pumpkin Soup

SERVES 4

As pumpkins arrive at markets in the fall, the cooler weather also makes it a great time of year for warm soup. Roasted pumpkin soup is a creamy, delicious, and healthy addition to fall meals.

1 Preheat water bath to 185°F (85°C) and oven to 400°F (200°C).

2 Place pumpkin, onion, garlic, and fennel on a tray and drizzle with olive oil. Place tray in the oven and roast for 10 minutes.

3 Transfer the contents of the tray to a plastic bag, add the stock, and seal using the immersion method or a vacuum sealer. Submerge the bag in the water bath and cook for 2 hours.

4 Optional: While the soup is cooking, combine all pesto ingredients and blend. Add enough basil to achieve a creamy consistency.

5 Remove the bag from the bath, blend, and serve. Garnish with pesto and/or roasted pumpkin seeds.

1 small pumpkin (about 2 cups), peeled and cubed

1 white onion, chopped

3 cloves garlic

1 fennel bulb, chopped

½ cup olive oil

2 cups vegetable stock

¼ cup roasted pumpkin seeds (optional)

PESTO (optional)

¼ cup olive oil

1 clove garlic

Bunch of fresh basil, cleaned and chopped

Refreshing Beet Salad

SERVES 4

Beets are delicious on their own and are great in a refreshing summer salad.

1 Preheat the water bath to 185°F (85°C).

2 Seal the beets in a plastic bag using the immersion method or a vacuum sealer, ensuring that they form a single layer. Submerge the bag in the water bath and cook for 30 minutes.

3 Remove bag of beets from the water bath and place into a pan of ice water to stop cooking and cool beets. Remove beets from bag and discard liquid.

4 To serve, line bottom of plate(s) with baby kale. Layer beets on top of kale, overlapping slightly. Top with crumbled blue cheese and chopped pecans. Sprinkle lightly with salt. Drizzle with olive oil and balsamic vinegar.

2 large or 3 medium beets, peeled and sliced in pieces ¼-inch thick

1 cup baby kale

¼ cup crumbled blue cheese

¼ cup chopped pecans

Sea salt to taste

Olive oil to taste

Balsamic vinegar to taste

Roasted Red Pepper Curry Soup

RECIPE BY
ZACH ADLEMAN

SERVES 6

The sous vide method works very well for soups because you won't burn them and you can't overcook them. You can also make several bags at a time and freeze the extras for later. Stored soups can be reheated in 15 minutes!

1 Torch or broil the red bell peppers until blackened, let cool, and then remove stem and seeds.

2 Preheat the water bath to 185°F (85°C).

3 Seal all the vegetables in a plastic bag using the immersion method or a vacuum sealer, ensuring that they form a single layer. Submerge the bag in the water bath and cook for 1 hour.

4 Place in a large pot with remaining ingredients, except red chili flakes and cilantro. Cook for 10 minutes. Blend or process until smooth.

5 Serve with salt and pepper to taste. Garnish with red chili flakes and cilantro.

4 red bell peppers

3 carrots, chopped

3 stalks celery, chopped

1 yellow onion, chopped

1 quart vegetable stock

1 (13.5-oz.) can coconut milk

1 Tbsp. red curry paste

2 cloves garlic, minced

Salt and pepper to taste

Red chili flakes, for garnish

Cilantro, for garnish

Scallops with Black Bean Salad

SERVES 2

Because shellfish are so delicate, small differences in cooking temperature have a big impact on the final texture. Leave nothing to chance by using sous vide. Scallops come out perfect at 126°F (52°C). This recipe is an example of cooking food that requires hotter temperatures first, then keeping them warm in the sous vide bath at lower temps.

1   Preheat your water bath to 194°F (90°C).

2   Seal the black beans, salt, pepper, garlic, and water in a plastic bag using the immersion method or a vacuum sealer. Submerge the bag in the water bath and cook for 5½ hours.

3   Reduce the water temperature to 140°F (60°C) by adding cold water or ice.

4   While the bath is cooling, add corn, red onion, and bell pepper to another bag. Seal the bag using the same method as in step 2. When the bath reaches the lower temperature, add the corn bag to the bath for 10 minutes.

5   Use the same method as in step 3 to lower the water temperature to 126°F (52°C).

6   While the bath is cooling, add scallops to a separate bag. Seal the bag using the same method as in step 2. When the bath reaches the lower temperature, add the scallop bag to the bath. Cook 15 minutes for small scallops or up to 30 minutes for large scallops.

7   Remove all 3 bags from the water bath. Open the bean and corn bags and pour contents into a colander to drain excess liquid. Transfer the drained corn and bean mixture to a mixing bowl and stir in olive oil and parsley. Drain the excess liquid from the scallop bag.

8   Melt butter in a pan over medium heat and lightly brown scallops in the butter.

9   To serve, add the bean and corn salad mixture to serving plates and top with scallops.

1 cup dried black beans

1 tsp. sea salt

1 tsp. black pepper

2 cloves garlic, chopped

3 cups water

1 cup kernels from fresh corn

¼ cup chopped red onion

½ red bell pepper, chopped

1 lb. scallops

¼ cup extra virgin olive oil

1 Tbsp. chopped fresh Italian parsley

2 Tbsp. unsalted butter

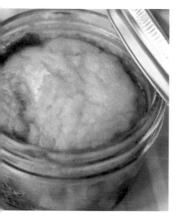

Desserts

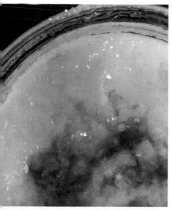

Cara Cara Orange Flan

SERVES 3

RECIPE BY
MOTOKO HAYASHI

Put a little summer back into winter with this Cara Cara orange flan. The refreshing orange flavor is rich and creamy without being overly sweet, like biting into a summertime orange. You may use any type of orange.

1 Preheat the water bath to 176°F (80°C).

2 In a small saucepan, boil the orange juice until it is reduced in half. Let it cool down.

3 In a bowl, beat the egg, egg yolks, and sugar. Mix in the reduced orange juice.

4 In another saucepan, heat the milk over medium heat until hot but not boiling. Add orange peel. Turn off heat, and let mixture steep for at least 15 minutes.

5 Slowly add the warm milk to the egg mixture. When it is cool, whisk in the heavy cream, then strain.

6 Carefully pour the mixture into the jars. Seal the jars but leave the ring slightly loose to allow air to escape, do not tighten completely. Add them to the water bath, ensuring the water level covers the jar. Cook for 60 minutes.

7 When it is done, cool the flan jars in the fridge. Pour honey on top of flan, garnish with orange supreme and orange peel before serving.

7 oz. Cara Cara orange juice

1 egg

2 egg yolks

¼ cup granulated sugar

½ cup whole milk, warm

Cara Cara orange peel from 1 orange

7 Tbsp. heavy cream

3 (8-oz.) canning jars

Honey, for garnish

Cara Cara orange, supreme (segmented), for garnish

Cara Cara orange peel, julienned, for garnish

Chocolate Espresso Cheesecake

SERVES 10

Sous vide makes cheesecake easy and convenient. The ability to make it in individual servings is an added plus. We took our Thanksgiving pumpkin cheesecake that has been a favorite, and substituted a few ingredients to make espresso chocolate.

1   Preheat water bath to 180°F (82°C).

2   In a medium mixing bowl, slowly add melted butter to crushed cookies, stirring well with a fork until all crumbs are consistently coated with the butter. Press the crumbs onto the bottom and about ⅓ of the way up the sides of canning jars until firm.

3   In a large mixing bowl, combine the cream cheese, sugar, and vanilla. Mix well with an electric mixer until smooth. Add the espresso and eggs. Continue mixing on high until smooth and creamy.

4   Pour the filling into the jars and fill to the bottom of the thread lines (about ¾ inch below the rim of the jar) Seal the jars but do not tighten completely. The rings should be slightly loose to allow air to escape. Add them to the water bath, ensuring the water level covers the jar. Cook for 2 hours.

5   Use tongs to remove the jars from the bath. Let them cool on the counter for 15 minutes, then place them in the refrigerator until completely cooled. Top with espresso beans and instant coffee and serve.

4 Tbsp. butter, melted

2 cups crushed chocolate sandwich cookies, preferably with chocolate filling

10 (8-oz.) canning jars

3 (8-oz.) packages cream cheese, at room temperature

1 cup sugar

1 tsp. vanilla

⅓ cup espresso, cooled to room temperature

3 eggs, at room temperature

Espresso beans, for garnish

Instant coffee, for garnish

Crème Brûlée

SERVES 6

Sous vide is an easy method for preparing a perfect crème brûlée. We love using canning jars for preparing individual servings.

1 Heat the heavy cream, milk, and vanilla in a saucepan over low heat, stirring continuously, and remove just before it boils. Set aside and let cool for 10 minutes.

2 While it is cooling, blend together the egg yolks, sugar, and salt using an immersion blender. While still blending, add the milk mixture to the egg mixture. Sieve the mixture and let settle until bubbles are nearly gone.

3 While the mixture is settling, preheat the water bath to 180°F (82°C).

4 Divide the mixture between 6 canning jars. Seal the jars but do not tighten completely. The ring should be slightly loose on each jar to allow air to escape. Add them to the water bath, ensuring the water level covers the jar. Cook for 70 minutes.

5 Remove from water bath and refrigerate until completely cool. Sprinkle sugar over the top of the custard and melt/caramelize with a small blowtorch. Do not use the Sansaire Searing Kit blowtorch for this as the flame is too hot and may crack the jars. Allow the caramelized crust to cool before serving.

2 cups heavy cream

⅔ cup whole milk

1 Tbsp. vanilla

6 egg yolks

¼ cup sugar, plus more for caramelization

Pinch of salt

6 (8-oz.) canning jars

Gâteau Invisible Aux Pommes

RECIPE BY
MOTOKO HAYASHI

SERVES 3

*For a stunning dessert, try our sous vide gâteau invisible aux pommes.
This delicate, low-calorie cake will be sure to impress your dinner guests.*

1 Preheat the water bath to 194.9°F (90.5°C).

2 Sift the cake flour and cinnamon.

3 In a large bowl, beat the egg, adding 1⅔ Tbsp. sugar gradually.

4 Add the milk gradually and then the melted butter.

5 Add in the flour mixture and mix well.

6 Put the sliced apples in the batter. Carefully mix, trying not to break the slices.

7 Prepare the jars by coating the inside of each jar with butter and cake flour. Tap to remove the excess flour.

8 Divide the batter between the prepared jars. Make sure the apple skins face to the outside and put them in a nice layer. Each cake should be 1¼ inches tall. Pour the excess batter over each jar.

9 Wipe off sides and tops of jars if there are any drips. Firmly tap jars on the counter to remove air bubbles. Seal the jars but do not tighten completely. The rings should be slightly loose to allow air to escape. Add them to the water bath, ensuring the water level covers the jars. Cook for 40 minutes.

10 Remove the jars from the water bath and transfer to a cooling rack. Carefully remove the lids. Cool to room temperature, then chill in the fridge for about 1 hour.

11 Remove cakes from each jar. Sprinkle 1 Tbsp. of granulated sugar on each cake. Torch until the surface gets brown and hard. If you don't have a torch, you may broil on high heat.

12 Sprinkle powdered sugar on top and serve.

---

7 Tbsp. cake flour, sifted, plus more for coating jars

⅛ tsp. cinnamon powder

1 egg, lightly beaten

4⅔ Tbsp. granulated sugar, divided

2⅓ Tbsp. whole or low-fat milk

2 Tbsp. unsalted butter, melted, plus more for coating jars

1 large honeycrisp or Fuji apple, unpeeled, cut in half and thinly sliced horizontally (3mm)

3 (16-oz.) canning jars

Powdered sugar, for garnish

Peach Berry Cobbler

SERVES 8

Sous vide is a easy method for preparing a perfect fruit cobbler. We love using canning jars for preparing individual servings.

1   Preheat the water bath to 195°F (90.5°C).

2   In a large bowl, gently mix peaches, blueberries, raspberries, ½ cup sugar, and cornstarch. Spoon mixture into the jars until ⅔ full.

3   In a large mixing bowl, combine the flour, ¼ cup sugar, baking soda, and salt.

4   In a separate bowl, combine the milk, sour cream, and butter. Add to dry ingredients to make the batter. Spoon the batter over the fruit, sprinkling the remaining sugar on top.

5   Seal the jars, but do not tighten completely. The rings should be slightly loose to allow air to escape. Add them to the water bath, ensuring the water level covers the jar. Cook for 3 hours.

6   Remove the jars from the bath and let cool to serving temperature. Optional: Brown the crust with a small blowtorch. Do not use the Sansaire Searing Kit torch for this as the flame is too hot and may crack the canning jars. Serve with whipped cream or vanilla ice cream, if desired.

4 ripe peaches, peeled and sliced

2 cups blueberries

1 cup raspberries

1 cup sugar, divided

2 Tbsp. cornstarch

8 (8-oz.) canning jars

1 cup self-rising flour

¼ tsp. baking soda

¼ tsp. salt

6 Tbsp. milk

¼ cup sour cream

2 Tbsp. butter, melted

Optional: Whipped cream or vanilla ice cream

Pumpkin Cheesecake

SERVES 10

Sous vide makes cheesecake easy and convenient. The ability to make it in individual servings is an added plus. This pumpkin cheesecake is a nice finish to fall or holiday dinners.

1   Preheat water bath to 180°F (82°C) and oven to 325°F (162.7°C).

2   In a medium mixing bowl, slowly add melted butter to graham cracker crumbs, stirring well with a fork until all crumbs are consistently coated with the butter. Press the crumbs onto the bottom and about ⅓ of the way up the sides of canning jars until firm.

3   Place uncovered jars in a baking pan or baking dish and fill pan or dish with hot water, but below thread line of the jars (about ¾ inch below the rim of each jar). Place in the oven for 15 minutes, remove and set jars aside to cool until you are ready to add filling.

4   In a large mixing bowl, combine the cream cheese, sugar, and vanilla. Mix well with an electric mixer until smooth. Add the pumpkin, eggs, cinnamon, nutmeg, and allspice. Continue mixing on high until smooth and creamy.

5   Pour the filling into the jars and fill to the bottom of the thread lines. Seal the jars but do not tighten completely. The rings should be slightly loose to allow air to escape. Add them to the water bath, ensuring the water level covers the jar. Cook in the water bath for 2 hours.

6   Use tongs to remove the jars from the bath. Let them cool on the counter for 15 minutes, then place them in the refrigerator until completely cooled. Top with whipped cream and serve.

4 Tbsp. butter, melted

2 cups graham cracker crumbs

10 (8-oz.) canning jars

3 (8-oz.) packages cream cheese, at room temperature

1 cup sugar

1 tsp. vanilla

1 cup canned pumpkin (not pie filling)

3 eggs, at room temperature

½ tsp. cinnamon

¼ tsp. nutmeg

¼ tsp. allspice

Whipped cream

Red Velvet Cake

SERVES 10

Individualized desserts are easy to make with sous vide. Red velvet cake is a delicious southern dessert with a rich cream cheese and pecan frosting. For our friends with nut allergies, it is easy to customize the single servings with substitutions like crushed peppermint.

1 Preheat your water bath to 203°F (95°C).

2 With an electric mixer, beat butter until smooth. Continue mixing while adding sugar, eggs, vanilla, vinegar, and food coloring. After the mixture is a consistent red color, continue mixing while slowly adding flour, buttermilk, cocoa, baking soda, and salt.

3 Grease and flour the canning jars. Pour batter in jars until ½ full to allow room for the cake to rise.

4 Seal the jars, but do not tighten completely. The rings should be slightly loose to allow air to escape. Add them to the water bath, ensuring the water level covers the jars. Cook for 3 hours.

5 Meanwhile, make the frosting. With an electric mixer, beat together butter and cream cheese until smooth. Continue mixing while adding powdered sugar and vanilla. Add chopped pecans (or chopped peppermint).

6 Remove the jars from the bath. Let them cool to room temperature before icing and serving the cakes.

CAKE

1 stick (½ cup) butter, at room temperature

1½ cups granulated sugar

4 medium or 3 large eggs, at room temperature

1 tsp. pure vanilla extract

1 Tbsp. white vinegar

½ oz. red food coloring

2½ cups flour, plus more for coating the jars

1 cup reduced-fat buttermilk

2 Tbsp. cocoa

1 tsp. baking soda

¼ tsp. salt

10 (8-oz.) canning jars

FROSTING

1 stick (½ cup) butter, at room temperature

1 (8 oz.) cream cheese, at room temperature

2 cups powdered sugar

1½ tsp. vanilla extract

1 cup coarsely chopped pecans. For nut allergies, substitute ½ cup chopped peppermint candy

S'more Flan

RECIPE BY
MOTOKO HAYASHI

SERVES 4

S'more flan is the perfect way to enjoy a classic dessert without the campfire. Velvety, creamy, and very chocolatey, but not too sweet, it leaves you wanting more.

1 In a small saucepan, mix milk and heavy cream. Heat until you see bubbles on the rim. Add a cinnamon stick, remove from the heat, and steep for 1 hour.

2 Remove the cinnamon stick, reheat the milk mixture, add the chopped chocolate, and stir every 10 minutes until the chocolate is fully incorporated. Cool down and add the eggs.

3 Preheat the water bath to 176°F (80°C.)

4 Coat the inside of the jars with butter and divide the mixture between them. Seal the jars but do not tighten completely. The rings should be slightly loose to allow air to escape. Add them to the water bath, ensuring the water level covers the jar. Cook for 1 hour.

5 Remove jars from the water bath with tongs. Cool the jars in the fridge.

6 To serve, loosen the sides of the flan by tipping the jar and inserting a small palette knife around the edges. Place a serving dish on top of the jar and turn upside down. Place 4–5 marshmallows on top of each flan, torch them, and sprinkle with graham cracker bits. Drizzle with chocolate sauce, if desired.

13½ Tbsp. whole milk

13½ Tbsp. heavy cream

1 cinnamon stick

7 oz. unsweetened 100% cacao chocolate, chopped

¼ cup granulated sugar

2 eggs, lightly beaten

4 (8-oz.) canning jars

Butter, for coating inside of jars

24 small or 12 large marshmallows, for garnish

Graham crackers, crumbled, for garnish

Optional: white chocolate sauce, for garnish

Zabaglione

SERVES 4

RECIPE BY
MOTOKO HAYASHI

For a romantic and beautiful after-dinner dessert, try sous vide zabaglione. Made with fresh fruit and a dash of Marsala, it makes for a simple and delicious treat.

1 Preheat the water bath to 149°F (65°C).

2 Place the egg yolks in a small bowl and gradually whisk in the powdered sugar. Whisk until the mixture is thick, then add the Marsala. Lightly whisk until the sugar dissolves.

3 Seal the egg mixture in a plastic bag using the immersion method or a vacuum sealer. Submerge the bag in the water bath. Cook for 20 minutes, shaking occasionally to ensure the egg mixture doesn't overcook.

4 To serve, place a dollop of warm zabaglione in the bottom of a goblet or glass. Top with a few berries, then repeat, ending with the berries. The dessert can be refrigerated for up to 6 hours before serving. Top with whipped heavy cream, if desired.

4 large egg yolks, beaten

¼ cup powdered sugar

¼ cup sweet Marsala wine

1 cup fresh strawberries, raspberries, blackberries, and/or blueberries

Optional: ½ cup heavy whipping cream, whipped

Beverages

Drinking Chocolate

SERVES 6

This drinking chocolate is rich and velvety, and sous vide makes preparation simple. The water bath will keep it warm until it's ready to be served. Chocolate and coffee enthusiasts will enjoy making this recipe with Sansaire and their favorite artisanal chocolates and espressos.

1 Preheat the water bath to 190°F (88°C).

2 Combine the milk, chocolate, brown sugar, and chili powder in the jar. Seal the jar, but do not tighten completely. The ring should be slightly loose to allow air to escape. Add it to the water bath, ensuring the water level covers the jar. Cook for 1 hour, opening and stirring every 10–15 minutes until the chocolate is fully melted and dissolved. Keep warm until it is served.

3 Remove the jar from the bath, stir, and serve. Add espresso shot(s) and sugar to taste.

3½ cups whole milk

10 oz. high-quality unsweetened dark chocolate, chopped

2 Tbsp. brown sugar

1 tsp. chili powder

Quart-size canning jar

Espresso and sugar, to taste

Hot Chocolate

SERVES 4

Sous vide makes velvety hot chocolate and keeps it warm until serving. Chocolate enthusiasts will enjoy making this recipe with Sansaire and their favorite artisanal chocolate.

1   Preheat the water bath to 190°F (88°C).

2   Combine the milk, chocolate, and brown sugar in the canning jar. Seal the jar, but do not tighten completely. The ring should be slightly loose to allow air to escape. Add it to the water bath, ensuring the water level covers the jar. Cook for 1 hour, opening and stirring every 10–15 minutes to ensure the chocolate is fully melted and dissolved. Keep warm until it is served.

3   Remove the jar from the bath, stir, and serve. Top with whipped cream, if desired.

4 cups whole milk

2 oz. high-quality unsweetened dark chocolate, chopped

½ cup brown sugar

1 (8-oz.) canning jar

Whipped cream (optional)

Infused Liquor

Infuse your favorite hard liquor (vodka, bourbon, rum, etc.) in a sous vide bath with Sansaire. We love it with lemon zest, orange zest, cherries, nuts, or cranberries. It is amazing how the flavors come through in the liquor, and it is fun to experiment with different combinations.

Option: Zest from 2 lemons, 1 orange, 1 grapefruit, or 3 limes

Option: ½ cup nuts

Option: ½ cup cranberries or sliced and peeled peaches

Pint-sized canning jar

1 pt. liquor(s) of your choice (vodka, rum, etc.)

1 Preheat the water bath to 135°F (57°C).

2 Add flavor(s) you are infusing to a canning jar. If you are using a citrus fruit zest, try to only get zest with as little of the white beneath the zest as possible. The white adds a bitter taste.

3 Fill the jar with the liquor of your choice (vodka, bourbon, rum, etc.).

4 Seal the jar but do not tighten completely. The ring should be slightly loose to allow air to escape. Add to the water bath, ensuring the water level covers the jar. Leave in water bath 1–3 hours.

5 Remove the jar from the bath and let cool to room temperature. Enjoy in a mixed drink or over ice.

Mulled Apple Cider

SERVES 4

Sous vide is not only a great way to make mulled apple cider, it's also a great way to keep it warm. Each quart-sized canning jar will make 4 servings of cider.

1 Preheat the water bath to 190°F (88°C).

2 Combine all of the ingredients and then divide into four jars. Seal the jars, but do not tighten completely. The rings should be slightly loose to allow air to escape. Add them to the water bath, ensuring the water level covers the jars. Leave in water bath for 1 hour. Can be left longer to be kept warm until it is served.

3 Remove the jars from the bath, strain, and serve. If spiking with rum, stir in before serving.

4 cups high-quality apple cider

2–3 cinnamon sticks

½ tsp. whole cloves

⅛ tsp. cinnamon

⅛ tsp. cardamom

⅛ tsp. coriander

Zest from 1 orange

Zest from 1 lemon

4 shots rum (optional)

4 (quart-sized) canning jars

Strawberry Daiquiri

SERVES 1

RECIPE BY
MOTOKO HAYASHI

Nothing says summer like an ice cold strawberry daiquiri. For a refreshing and delicious beverage that isn't overly sweet, our strawberry daiquiri is a must-have at any summer gathering.

INFUSED RUM

1 Preheat the bath to 135°F (57°C).

2 Seal the rum, lemon and lime juice and zest, and strawberries in a plastic bag using the immersion method or a vacuum sealer. Submerge the bag in the water bath and cook for 2 hours.

3 Remove the bag and submerge it in an ice water bath to chill completely. Strain the rum, discarding the peels. Reserve strawberries. Pour the infused rum into a clean bottle. Chill well.

4 Use a blender to puree the cooked strawberries and chill.

COCKTAIL

1 Dip a chilled cocktail glass in sugar to decorate the top of the glass.

2 Put all of the ingredients in a cocktail shaker (except strawberries and lime), shake well, and strain.

3 Pour mixture into the cocktail glass. Garnish with fresh strawberries and a lime slice. Serve immediately.

INFUSED RUM
(Makes about 750 ml)

750 ml clear rum

Zest and juice from 4 lemons

Zest and juice from 4 limes

1 pint fresh, ripe strawberries, stemmed and quartered

COCKTAIL
(Makes 1 cocktail)

Sugar for rim

2 oz. infused rum

¾ oz. simple syrup

¾ oz. strawberry puree

Ice

Fresh strawberries, halved, for garnish

Lime, sliced, for garnish

About the Chefs and Photographer

Zachary Michel Adleman

Zachary Michel Adleman began his culinary career taping cooking shows that he'd watch after school when he was twelve. His father helped foster a love for food, from crawfish boils to gourmet weeknight meals to three-day cooking affairs over the holidays. He has only ever worked in kitchens, holding every position from dishwasher to line cook to head chef. He graduated from the Escoffier Culinary Institute in 2013 and currently is Chef de cuisine at The 4580 in Boulder, Colorado.

Geoff Barker

Geoff Barker is a self-taught home cook with a passion to create and deliver high-quality meals to his family and friends. His love of food started while on a student exchange to Malaysia in the late '90s and has grown in the subsequent years. He thoroughly enjoys experimenting with new flavors, textures, and techniques; he learns something new every time he steps into the kitchen. He finds that quality ingredients are key to producing great results. He supports local businesses in the purchase of all his fresh produce and small goods. He is honored and humbled to be a contributor to this cookbook and trusts that you will enjoy recreating the recipes he developed in his home kitchen.

Motoko Hayashi

Motoko Hayashi is a very creative and artistic chef who pays close attention to details and makes dishes that are a feast for the eyes as well as the palate. Plating is her passion and she believes that people "eat with their eyes" like her grandmother always told her. With that in mind, she strives to create divine dishes with seasonal ingredients that are meaningful to the people who eat them. As a lifelong learner and a recipe tester, she enjoys the opportunity to experiment in the challenging environment of the culinary field and to continue to grow her skills and technical acumen. She is also a personal chef and an owner of a glass production company. When she is not cooking, she creates glass arts in her own glass studio and grows vegetables and herbs in her own garden in Seattle, where she lives with her glass artist husband and their cute French bulldog.

Jessica Cnossen

Jessica Cnossen is a Seattle-based lifestyle photographer, specializing in food imagery. She picked up her first camera six years ago and hasn't put it down since. Her style can be described as bright and clean, using color and texture to bring out the details in her work. Outside the studio, she enjoys spending quality time with her husband, family, and two energetic pugs, Leonard and Lorenzo.

Index

A

Asian Inspired Steak Salad 159
Asparagus with Sous Vide Egg, Pancetta, and Hollandaise 43

B

Baccala 9
Bacon and Eggs with Hash Browns 44
Baked Camembert Cheese 10
Banana Nut Oatmeal 47
Beef Brisket 71
Beet Poke 160
Breakfast Mushi-Pan (Savory Steamed Muffins) 48
Brioche Pain Perdu Jarred 51
Brussels Sprouts with Bacon and Garlic 125
Buffalo Chicken Wings 13
Buttermilk Pork Cutlet with Sweet Potato Mash and Greens 72

C

Cajun Stuffing 126
Calamari and Octopus Mediterranean Couscous 75
Cara Cara Orange Flan 185
Cauliflower and Romanesco with Indian Spices 129
Chawan Mushi-Pan (Savory Japanese Egg Custard) 14
Cheeseburger, The 195 119
Cheese Mushi-Pan (Cheese Steamed Muffins) 52
Chicken Burger 76
Chicken-Fried Steak with Maple Bourbon Brown Gravy 55
Chicken Salad 163
Chicken Wraps 79
Chilean Sea Bass 80
Chilled Carrot Soup 164
Chocolate Espresso Cheesecake 186
Coffee Pork Chops 83
Cola Pork Belly 17
Cornish Game Hens 84
Cranberry Sauce 133
Crème Brûlée 189
Crispy Skin Duck with Green Mango Salad 167

D

Daikon Cheesesteak 18
Drinking Chocolate 205

E

Eggs Benedict 56
Eggy Mash Jar 59

F

Fava Bean and Asparagus Risotto 134
Fried Egg Yolks 60
Fried Jasmine Rice 87

G

Garlic and Cambozola Cheese Spread 21
Garlic Hummus 22
Gâteau Invisible Aux Pommes 190
Green Chili Corn 96

H

Hamburger 88
Homemade Italian Sausage 91
Hot Chocolate 206

I

Infused Liquor 209
Infused Oil 137

J

Jasmine Rice 145

K

Kamo Roast: Japanese-Style Duck Breast 92

L

Lemon Black Pepper Infused Oil 138
Lemongrass Tofu Steak 95
Lemon Pepper Chicken over Kale Salad 168
Lobster Salad 171

M

Matcha Mushi-Pan (Green Tea Steamed Muffins) 63
Mozzarella Cheese Stuffed Meatballs 25
Mulled Apple Cider 210
Mushroom and Ham Flan 64
Mushroom Risotto 141

O

Onion Farce (Stuffed Onions) 26
Orange-Infused Maple Syrup 51
Oyster Poche (Poached Oyster) with Ponzu Gelee 29

P

Pasta Sauce 142
Peach Berry Cobbler 193

Pearl Onions with Raisins 145
Pollo Poblano with Green Chili Corn 96
Pork Belly Sliders 30
Pork Green Chili 99
Potato Leek Soup 172
Potato Mash 146
Preserved Lemon 149
Preserved-Lemon Chicken 100
Pumpkin Cheesecake 194
Pumpkin Soup 175

R

Rack of Lamb with Sous Vide Infused Mint Butter 103
Rainbow Carrot Salad 150
Ramen Eggs 153
Red Velvet Cake 197
Refreshing Beet Salad 176
Ribeye Steak Nachos 33
Rib Fillet with Potato Gratin, Greens, and Bercy Glaze 104
Roasted Cipollini Onions with Honey Balsamic Vinegar Sauce 154
Roasted Red Pepper Curry Soup 179
Roast Pork Belly, Vegetables, Sauvignon Mustard Sauce 107

S

Salmon Yuan-Yaki 108
Scallops and Fennel with Yuzu Kosho Sauce 111
Scallops with Black Bean Salad 180
Scotch Eggs 67
Sea Scallop Tartare 34
Sesame Tofu Steak 112
S'more Flan 198
Steak with Wasabi Sauce 115
Strawberry Daiquiri 213
Stuffed Baby Calamari in Tomato Sauce 37

T

Thai Coconut Curry with Tofu 116
The 195 Cheeseburger 119
Turkey Breast 120

V

Vegan Stuffed Artichoke 38

W

Walnut Chili Oil 130

Z

Zabaglione 201